ISBN 978-0-282-52421-0
PIBN 10854834

English
Français
Deutsche
Italiano
Español
Português

www.forgottenbooks.com

Mythology Photography **Fiction**
Fishing Christianity **Art** Cooking
Essays Buddhism Freemasonry
Medicine **Biology** Music **Ancient
Egypt** Evolution Carpentry Physics
Dance Geology **Mathematics** Fitness
Shakespeare **Folklore** Yoga Marketing
Confidence Immortality Biographies
Poetry **Psychology** Witchcraft
Electronics Chemistry History **Law**
Accounting **Philosophy** Anthropology
Alchemy Drama Quantum Mechanics
Atheism Sexual Health **Ancient History**
Entrepreneurship Languages Sport
Paleontology Needlework Islam
Metaphysics Investment Archaeology
Parenting Statistics Criminology
Motivational

HERACLITUS

BY PHILIP WHEELWRIGHT

PRINCETON, NEW JERSEY

PRINCETON UNIVERSITY PRESS

1959

To
my first teacher
Elizabeth D. Meeker
in gratitude

PREFACE

"There is a harmony in the bending back, as in the case of the bow and the lyre." Thus Heraclitus observes in Fragment 117; and the complementing virtues of marksmanship and lyrical sensitivity must both be courted in any attempt to rediscover and freshly interpret the extraordinary subtleties and depths of his ancient wisdom.

The present book was begun during a special leave of absence granted me by the University of California at Riverside; it was brought to virtual completion while I was the visiting William Allan Neilson research professor at Smith College. I am grateful to both institutions for the opportunities thus provided.

Five professorial friends have generously put their scholarship at my disposal as needed: Professor Harry Carroll of Pomona College; Mr. W. Dyfrig Evans, while he was a visiting member of the U.C.R. Classics Department; Professor Alfred Young Fisher of Smith College; Professor Philip Merlan of Scripps College; and Professor Wolfgang Yourgrau, at present the Cowling Visiting Professor of Philosophy at Carleton College. The last named (last only by alphabetical accident) has brought his special knowledge of the philosophy of science and his familiarity with Greek language and literature jointly to bear upon the problems of ancient science discussed in Chapter III. I am indebted no less, although in different respects, to Miss Harriet Anderson of the Princeton University Press, for her constant exercise of sound judgment, good taste, and technical proficiency during the months of our collaboration; to Dr. Gertrud Neuwirth of the University of Frankfurt for varied assistance; to Miss Dorothea Berry, reference librarian at U.C.R.; and to my wife, who has labored long with the proofs at their successive stages.

Finally, my gratitude is real although less specifically focussed toward those students in my ancient philosophy courses, recently at the University of California at Riverside and earlier at Dartmouth College, who have shared in the excitement of rediscovering Heraclitus with me, and whose responsiveness has helped to confirm my abiding conviction of the philosopher's greatness.

P. W.

University of California
at Riverside
August 1959

CONTENTS

PREFACE   vii

INTRODUCTION   3

    I. THE WAY OF INQUIRY   19

   II. UNIVERSAL FLUX   29

  III. THE PROCESSES OF NATURE   37

  IV. HUMAN SOUL   58

   V. IN RELIGIOUS PERSPECTIVE   68

  VI. MAN AMONG MEN   83

 VII. RELATIVITY AND PARADOX   90

VIII. THE HIDDEN HARMONY   102

APPENDICES   111

    CONCORDANCE OF FRAGMENT NUMBERS 112

    APPENDIX A. NOTES TO THE CHAPTERS 113

    APPENDIX B. NOTES ON THE FRAGMENTS 130

    APPENDIX C. REJECTED FRAGMENTS 157

    APPENDIX D. BIBLIOGRAPHY 159

GENERAL INDEX   173

INDEX OF PRINCIPAL GREEK WORDS   178

HERACLITUS

INTRODUCTION

THE sixth century B.C. was a time of philosophical ferment in many places. If we do not draw the boundaries of the century too exactly, we may include within it, with a fairly high degree of probability, such widely separated and often diverse philosophers as Lao-tze in China, Zoroaster (more properly Zarathustra) in Iran, the anonymous authors of several of the Upanishads in India, the Deutero-Isaiah in Exilic Israel, and a number of different and sometimes sharply opposed individualists in various parts of the Greek-speaking world. It is a mystery, which no one has succeeded in explaining, why there should have been such a nearly simultaneous concentration of philosophical activities in countries that appear to have had no direct connection with each other. At all events, our present concern is with one particular aspect of this general manifestation; and the reader may observe or ignore, at his discretion, the somewhat analogous developments occurring at the same time in different parts of the then civilized world.

So far as Greece is concerned, there are virtually no evidences of anything that could properly be called philosophy existing in earlier times. There are momentary flashes of philosophical insight in Hesiod's *Works and Days*, in the so-called Homeric Hymns (whatever their dates may have been), and in the fragmentary sayings attributed to Orpheus and his followers; but in none of them is there any intellectual coherence or any interest in finding a method for distinguishing truth from error. The ancient saying cited by Plato, that "God holds the beginning and the end, as well as the middle, of all existing things,"[1] has been attributed to the legendary Orpheus, and it contains an arresting thought—especially if, as was usual with the Greeks, the ideas of beginning, end, and middle carried not only temporal but also moral meanings, connoting respectively (1) principle, (2) goal or fulfillment, and (3) balance or proportion. But the quotation

[3]

stands virtually alone; most of the other early Orphic sayings are more burdened with mythological assumptions, and none of them reveals so clear an intellectual focus. In the gnomic poets of the seventh century, too, there are a few scattered utterances that show flashes of philosophic insight, but here again the occasional sense of significance is sporadic, unmethodical, and unpromising.

PHILOSOPHY IN IONIA

The first independent and sustained attempt to work out a philosophic view of the world is found in Ionia, to the east of Greece proper, in the sixth century. Here, in the seaport town of Miletus, Thales and his two successors, Anaximander and Anaximenes, began to ask questions in a new way. Described by ancient writers as "physiologues,"[2] because they were seeking a reasoned understanding (*logos*) of nature (*physis*), they formulated—apparently for the first time in the Western world—the two great scientific-philosophical questions of What and How. The two things they chiefly wanted to know were: "What is the primary stuff of which the world is constituted?" and "How do the changes take place that bring about its manifold appearances?" Previously the nearest that the Greek mind had come to launching such inquiries was to ask not "What?" but "Who?" and not "How?" but "With what purpose and intention?" The historical importance of Thales, as founder of the Milesian school, does not rest on his somewhat primitive and naïve theory that all things are transformations of water, nor on the legends of his wizardry and absent-mindedness, but on the fact that he began the work of seeking for explanations of the natural world within the natural world itself. An understanding and formulation of the two questions—"What is basically real?" and "How does change come about?"—is far more important, both for clarity of mind and in terms of subsequent influence, than any possible answers that can ever, then or now, be given to them.

Thales' greatest follower, Anaximander, made an attempt to answer the first of these questions by his conception of a boundless reservoir of potential qualities,[3] out of which warmth or coldness, health or sickness, light or dark, and so on, would emerge into actual existence at certain times and places and subsequently would be reabsorbed into that boundless cosmic reservoir (to speak, as one must, metaphorically) in which all things exist merely as potentials. Anaximander answered the second question by his conception—partly biological, partly ethical, partly religious—of what can most nearly be described as existential penance. "Things make reparation," he declared, "and therein do justice to one another according to the order of time."[4] This is his one preserved statement of how a change from one quality to another —say from warmth to coolness in the atmosphere—comes about. The meaning can best be understood by looking at it in two perspectives successively. In biological perspective we can—on the analogy of an organism that grows, reproduces, and dies—regard a quality, such as summer heat, as coming into being, achieving full growth, and then, after a suitable time, making way for the opposite quality—in this case winter cold—which is to be conceived as going in its turn through the same life-cycle. In ethico-religious perspective the situation can be conceived through the typically Greek idea of *hybris,* which can be roughly translated *flagrant self-assertion*. Now what Anaximander's metaphysical imagination has done is to envisage the process of flagrant self-assertion together with its self-terminating outcome as applying not only to human life but to all existing entities whatsoever. The light of day, when it has asserted itself by existing for enough hours, must at length yield to the conflicting claims of the darkness of night, which has been lurking in a merely potential state, awaiting, as it were, its chance of bursting into actuality.

Anaximander's doctrine, so far as it deals with the problem of change, is a forerunner of Heraclitus' doctrine in two respects. In the first place it conceives of change in purely qualitative terms. That is to say, change is not, as it is for modern physical science, primarily spatial motion, or even measurable by some device of spatial motion or spatial distancing. It is essentially what it appears to be—the disappearance of one perceptual quality (say felt warmth or visible brightness or audible noise) while another and contrary quality (respectively, coolness, darkness, or silence) takes its place. Change is an ontological passage from contrary to contrary—from one perceptible state of being to its opposite. In the second place Anaximander conceives of the relation between contraries as in some sense a periodic interchange, exemplifying a cyclic and somewhat rhythmic principle— "according to the order of time."

Anaximenes, too, the last of the three Milesian philosophers, although generally regarded as inferior to his immediate predecessor in philosophical stature, nevertheless offers two teachings that make him a significant forerunner of Heraclitus. First, he takes the primary physical reality to be air; for, as he argues in one of his few surviving fragments, "As our souls, being air, hold us together, so do breath and air encompass the entire universe."[5] His second thesis—of great historical importance in that it opened the way to the later employment of quantitative concepts in physical science—is the interpretation of change in terms of serial order. Every occurrence in nature, he holds, is a result and outward show of the rarefaction or condensation of air. Rarefaction eventually produces fire; condensation at successive stages produces cloud, water, mud, earth, and rock. Here evidently is something roughly analogous to Heraclitus' "way up and way down," and the question suggests itself whether Heraclitus may have been influenced by Anaximenes, or whether both philosophers may have drawn upon a common source; but unfortunately there is no evidence on which an answer can rest.

One further Ionian philosopher, not from Miletus and

quite distinct from the trio just mentioned, invites consideration because of his possible bearing upon the thought of
Heraclitus. Xenophanes was born in the Ionian town of
Colophon, probably about a generation before Heraclitus, and
he appears to have spent much of his time as a traveling min-
strel, taking as the themes of his songs philosophical and
religious ideas. Although his utterances are of a more open
kind, less gnomic and paradoxical, than those of Heraclitus,
there is a certain eloquent bitterness to be found in both
philosophers, particularly as directed against prevailing
stupidities of belief. In Xenophanes' case the doctrine that is
especially under attack is the popular mythology of the
Olympian gods. The gods, taken plurally, he denounces as
fictions in anthropomorphic guise. If horses could draw, he
remarks, they "would portray their gods in the shape of
horses, and oxen in the shape of oxen." We are victims, he
could have said, using Bacon's later figure, of idols of the
tribe. Is there any escape from such idols? Yes, Xenophanes
thinks, there is. We must practice the art of ridding our
highest conceptions of all accidental, trivial, and self-mirror-
ing qualities. As a result he arrives at the first clear statement
of monotheism, so far as is known, in the West. "There is one
God," he declares, "the greatest among gods and men, not at
all like mortals in form or in thought." To be sure, since we
regard this supreme One as divine, we must conceive Him
as more excellent, not less so, than mortals, and this means
that He must be somehow capable of thought and perception,
for an entirely unconscious entity would not be worthy of
reverence. Such thought and perception must not be conceived as dependent on organs, however; "it is in his entirety
that he sees, in his entirety that he thinks, and in his entirety
that he hears." Nor does he have to exert himself in order
to bring things about; "he accomplishes everything by the
sheer thought of his mind."[6] He is, in short, the transcendent
unifier and the principle of unity that resides amidst all change
and multiplicity. Xenophanes has thus taken an important

[7]

and apparently an original step in setting up the concept of a God divested of human attributes. His critical approach to philosophy through the religious problem complements the Milesian critical approach through the problem of nature. Metaphysics, or what we may call more precisely cosmology, involves both approaches; they provide respectively the polar concepts of the One and the Many.

PYTHAGOREANISM AND ELEATICISM

Two other philosophies, the Pythagorean and the Eleatic, need to be mentioned as partly contemporaneous with Heraclitus, and as just possibly having had some oblique influence upon him, although this is doubtful. Granted that both philosophies reached their peak of influence after the probable date of Heraclitus' death, nevertheless in their earlier phases they may perhaps have been known to him in indirect ways. I am not arguing that this was so, but it is just as well to reckon with the possibility.

There is certainly no evidence or likelihood that Heraclitus had ever been influenced by Pythagoras directly. The two derogatory remarks, of doubtful authenticity, which he was later quoted as having made about the older philosopher may be found as Frs. 128 and 136 in Appendix C. If he actually did make them, it must be admitted that he showed neither understanding nor sympathy toward Pythagoras and his teaching. Most of Pythagoras' teaching, moreover, was done in Italy, in the little city of Crotona where he had established a brotherhood for the further pursuit of philosophy; and although he was probably older than Heraclitus by a generation, it is improbable that his views, which were carefully guarded, would have been carried to Ionia within a few years or decades. Finally, the two men, to judge by the available evidence, were sharply different in intellectual temperament. Pythagoras' doctrine, compounded of mysticism, mathematics, cosmology, and music, is so alien to our current preconceptions that its original intelligibility is difficult to recapture; and while Heraclitus would not have opposed it for the same reasons as we, he was too fiercely individualistic to accept any such teaching from another, even if he had come in contact with it.

On the other hand, there is an ancient tradition that Heraclitus had been a pupil of the Pythagorean philosopher Hippasus of Metapontum. The tradition is too shaky to stand as evidence, however; for some scholars regard Hippasus as having postdated Heraclitus, and moreover Iamblichus in his *Life of Pythagoras* discredits his Pythagoreanism. The two firm facts about Hippasus are that he had been at one time a member of the Pythagorean brotherhood, and that like Heraclitus he believed that the universe is in a state of incessant change and that it consists of fire as its primal element.[7] But whether he held the belief ahead of Heraclitus or drew it from him, is impossible to determine; and in any case so simple and general a congruity might, of course, have been coincidental.

The problem of Heraclitus' relation to Parmenides of Elea again involves an uncertain question of comparative dates. A majority of scholars have supposed that Parmenides wrote his long poem on truth and appearance after Heraclitus had published his treatise on nature. Two main reasons for the conventional dating may be noticed. First, there is the evidence of Plato's dialogue, the *Parmenides*, in which Socrates as a young man is represented as conversing with the aged Parmenides. Since Socrates was born in 469 B.C., the conversation (assuming that Plato did not invent it) would probably have taken place not earlier than about 450. In that case, whatever Parmenides' exact age may have been at the time, it would seem probable that the writing of his philosophy would have taken place after, rather than before, the turn of the century, which was the time at which Heraclitus is said to have flourished. Secondly, there is the passage supposed by a number of scholars to refer to Heraclitus, in which Parmenides warns against "undisciplined crowds who hold that *to be* and *not to be* are the same and yet not the same, and that the way of things everywhere is παλίντροπος."[8] Although, as Zeller has pointed out, Heraclitus does not in any extant Fragment say that being and not-being are the same and not the same (and, incidentally, he can hardly be well described as an undisciplined crowd), yet the word παλίντροπος ("bending back," "tension between opposites") is so distinctive as to suggest the possibility of a deliberate reference to Fragment 117, where Heraclitus uses the same word.

Nevertheless, despite these rather strong evidences, it is not certain that Parmenides' writing postdates that of Heraclitus. A scholar of independent mind, Karl Reinhardt, has argued with much learning and ingenuity that Heraclitus may have flourished as much as two decades after Parmenides, and that his theory of an ever-changing universe arose in reaction against Parmenides' unworkable theory that change is unreal.[9] Parmenides had argued that an intelligible view of the world is only possible to one who regards it as undifferentiated and static; Heraclitus (if Reinhardt's redating is accepted) could be interpreted as retorting to Parmenides' oversimple theory with the countertheory that intelligibility is to be found only in what is multiple and changing—only in strife itself. To be sure, Reinhardt's dating has not won wide acceptance; nevertheless the possibility of Heraclitus' having reacted against Parmenides in the manner described should doubtless be kept open.

HERACLITUS

Heraclitus himself was a native of Ephesus, an Ionian city some twenty-five miles north of Miletus and inland from the sea, and he is said by Diogenes Laertius to have flourished there in the sixty-ninth Olympiad, which would be roughly equivalent to 504-500 B.C. His family was an ancient and noble one in the district, and Heraclitus inherited from them some kind of office, partly religious, partly political, the exact nature of which is not clear, but it involved among other things supervision of sacrifices. Doubtless such an office was not congenial to a man of his impatient temperament, and he resigned it in favor of a younger brother. The banishment of his friend Hermodorus by a democratic government increased a natural antagonism to the masses and confirmed him in his philosophical withdrawal. So much is virtually all that can be known about Heraclitus with reasonable probability. Diogenes Laertius' short essay on him in *Lives and Opinions of Eminent Philosophers*[10] is a rather scatterbrained affair, and there is no reason to take seriously his fantastic account of the philosopher's death by self-burial in a cow stall in a vain effort to cure an attack of dropsy. Such improbable tales were not uncommon about ancient "wise men," and Diogenes provides more than his share of them; quite possibly their origin was aetiological in that they grew out of popular misunderstandings of something that the philosopher had taught. In the case of Heraclitus we cannot even know whether it is true that he died of dropsy; the story could easily have been a figment suggested by his remark, "It is death for souls to become water."

In temperament and character Heraclitus was said to have been gloomy, supercilious, and perverse. Diogenes calls him a hater of mankind, and says that this characteristic led him to live in the mountains, making his diet on grass and roots, a regimen which brought on his final illness. Such an account, however, is of the sort that could easily have been invented out of a general view of the philosopher's character. At any rate, Heraclitus was certainly no lover of the masses, and his declaration, "To me one man is worth ten thousand if he is first-rate" (Fr. 84), makes it evident that he was not one to suffer fools gladly. He would have understood and approved of Nietzsche's definition of the truly aristocratic man as one whose thoughts, words, and deeds are inwardly motivated by a "feeling of distance."[11] However, to call him a pessimist and compare him to Schopenhauer, as more than one interpreter of his writings has done, is to treat him in a misleadingly one-sided manner. Pessimism, where it is a philosophy and not just a mood, affirms the doctrine that there is more evil in the world than good, or that the evil is somehow more fundamental or more real. Heraclitus does not commit himself to so partisan a statement. His doctrine is rather that good and evil are two sides of the same reality, as are up and down, beauty and ugliness, life and death. The wise man attempts to set his mood by looking unflinchingly at both sides of the picture, not at either the bright or the dark alone.

So far as is known, Heraclitus was the author of a single book. Diogenes Laertius describes its subject-matter as "on nature," adding that it was divided into three sections—on the universe, on statecraft, and on theology. According to that same sketchy biographer Heraclitus dedicated his book in the temple of Artemis and deposited a scroll of it there—a fairly usual practice in ancient Greece.[12] The virtually unanimous opinion of ancient writers is that the book was hard to understand, and its author was frequently described by such epithets as the Dark, the Obscure, and the Riddling.[13] Diogenes Laertius suggests that the obscurity may have been deliberate, in order that none might read the book who had not honored it with a suitable degree of intellectual effort. Since the Fragments that survive from it consist mostly of single sentences, we have little or no direct evidence as to how the various ideas in it were assembled, but their pithiness and profundity are still unmistakable, even though the original contexts have been lost.

EXPRESSION AND PRESUPPOSITION

Since Heraclitus is one of the subtlest, most impatient, and most paradoxical of philosophers, any attempt to reduce his doctrine to a few plain propositions could only result in distortion and caricature. Interpretations of his meaning have to be somewhat tentative, left open to the qualifications and reformulations that a thoughtful reader may wish to make as he reflects further on some of the dark sayings. There is always the danger, with Heraclitus as with any other ancient philosopher, of interpreting the ideas and the words—or someone's chosen translation of the words—on the basis of contemporary presuppositions and distinctions, such as may have been absent, or nearly so, from the thought of an earlier age. We become subject, more than we are aware, to idols of the theater.[14] In particular there are three modes of distinguishing, which seem quite natural to us today, but which are relied on to a far lesser degree in the thought and expression of Heraclitus: our grammatical distinction among parts of speech, our logical distinction between the concrete and the abstract, and our epistemological distinction between subject and object.

The distinction among parts of speech is less pronounced in the Greek language than in the Latin and its Western successors. Accordingly it is often impossible for a translator to find in a modern language the precise equivalent of some word or idiom in the Greek. The difficulty, indeed, is more than grammatical, it is ontological; for it concerns the *kind of being* which the different types of words are designed to indicate. Of particular interest are the three word-types of noun, adjective, and verb, together with the three modes of being for which they respectively stand—things, qualities, and events. The correlation is not absolute, to be sure; for we have to remind ourselves occasionally that an abstract noun such as "justice" does not indicate a thing, and that the copula "is" lacks the usual semantic properties of other verbs. But in general our contemporary Western languages keep a fairly steadfast distinction among the three types—nouns standing for things, adjectives standing for qualities, and verbs standing for actions and events.

Now in the thought of Heraclitus, abetted by the comparative fluidity of the Greek language, the linguistic distinction and correspondingly the ontological distinction are somewhat less firm. Consider Fr. 22, for instance: "Cool things become warm, the warm grows cool; the moist dries, the parched becomes moist." Is Heraclitus speaking here about things or about qualities? The subject of the first clause is neuter plural preceded by the definite article, while in each of the three remaining clauses the subject term is a neuter singular without the article. Yet it is evident that the four clauses are parallel, and that the four subject terms are offered as representing parallel situations. The answer seems to be that scarcely any distinction was recognized between cool and warm things and the resident qualities of coolness and warmth. It was not until a century and a half later that Aristotle delineated the difference explicitly and showed what the intellectual penalty for ignoring it would be—a point to be developed in Chapter II. And in Heraclitus' thought not only the ideas of thing and quality but also those of event and quality tend to coalesce and become confused. The latter confusion tends to be encouraged by the readiness of the Greek language to employ the infinitive of a verb preceded by the neuter definite article. Where such a construction appears in Fr. 10, for instance, I have translated it "to be temperate," although a more literal translation would be "*the* to be temperate," and doubtless the sense of action (or potential action), quality, and thinghood were all present in it.

The coalescence between concrete and abstract is especially evident in Heraclitus' central image-idea of fire. Regarding Frs. 28, 29, 30, and 32, the question has been raised: Is he speaking about actual physical fire, which burns and flares, or is he employing a picturesque symbol to denote incessant change? No one-sided answer can be maintained without doing violence to the doctrine; the true answer has to be— both! Goethe, who evinced a lively interest in Heraclitus after Schleiermacher had presented him with a first collection of some of the Fragments, defines a genuine symbol as a particular instance which is coalescent with a universal and which thereby plays a unique role by revealing, in a way that no other particular could quite do, the nature of that more general something.[15] Fire, in Heraclitus' doctrine, is a symbol in something very like the Goethean sense. It is the yellow, flaming, heat-giving actuality while at the same time it stands for the Heraclitean principle of universal unrelenting change.

The third type of coalescence that is more natural to earlier methods of thinking than to our own is found in the coalescence of subject and object, or knower and known, or thinker and thing thought. A comparison of Frs. 119 and 120 is instructive in this regard. Each of these Fragments begins with the same three words, stating that wisdom (more literally, the quality of being wise) is one, but they amplify the idea in different directions. Fr. 119 identifies this unitary wisdom with the divine power that is active in all things, and thus has a somewhat objective reference; Fr. 120 identifies the same unitary wisdom with the power of knowing that cosmic intelligence, and thereby has a somewhat subjective reference. Such is the distinction that tends to suggest itself to the modern reader, one of whose most complacent assumptions is that he knows how to draw the line between what is objective and what is subjective, and that except in certain rare and abnormal cases there is no difficulty in doing so. To an ancient thinker, on the other hand, whose mind would not have been conditioned (as ours has largely been) by the postulates of Cartesian dualism, the division between objective and subjective wore no such appearance of clarity and finality. The idea of what might belong to the one and what might belong to the other would vary according to mood and circumstance, and no precise question about it was ever raised. Heraclitus shows at times (as in Frs. 11, 13, 15, and 16) a strong, but not a clear, feeling for the question; Parmenides acknowledges its importance by building his poem upon a contrast between the way of truth and the way of opinion; but it was not until the age of the Sophists that Greek Philosophy had acquired the vocabulary and the dialectical skill to handle the question firmly. The Sophists' own answer to it erred on the side of excessive subjectivity, and Plato in attempting to correct their error produced a certain amount of metaphysical muddle. Aristotle's ingenious and promising attempt to solve the riddle[16] is disappointingly incomplete, and in general it may be said that Greek philosophy never succeeded in grappling with the problem adequately. Perhaps it is just as well. A seeker after truth will fare best if he tries, whatever the intellectual inconveniences, to keep his categories and his ontological premises somewhat flexible. Such flexibility is what gives to much early Greek philosophy, and particularly to that of Heraclitus, its characteristic resilience and vitality.

These three kinds of semantic coalescence are not peculiar to the thought of the Greeks. With variations in detail they are to be found in much of the philosophical thought of ancient India, Iran, and China too. Because of them many of the remarks in the *Upanishads*, the *Zend-Avesta*, and the *Tao Teh Ching* appear dark and riddling, or on the other hand naïve and superficial. In their clarity of thought, their sharpness of imagery, and their economy of ontological assumptions, the sayings of Heraclitus are more akin to the *Tao Teh Ching* than to the religio-philosophical documents of India and Iran, although they are doubtless more like these in their prophetic tone. In any case the lucidity that characterizes most of Heraclitus' sayings (despite the ancient cliché to the contrary) must be understood on its own terms. It is sometimes subtly different from what passes for lucidity at the present day, and such difference is at bottom a difference in certain basic thought-forms, of which I have indicated three of the most prominent. A first step in trying to understand any writer, and particularly an ancient writer, is to exercise our "negative capability,"[17] bracketing off our habitual ways of joining and distinguishing ideas wherever such ways differ from the writer's own. This step is especially demanded by the flowing and often paradoxical thought of Heraclitus, and the cost of ignoring it would be a misleading oversimplification.

ON TEXT AND INTERPRETATION

The problem of resurrecting the thought of an ancient writer whose remains consist only of quoted fragments will have two main phases. There is the question of the authenticity of particular fragments, and there is the question of how to interpret the fragments that are accepted. Once the authenticity of a fragment has been established, or at least accepted upon reasonable grounds, the question of interpretation may arise in any or all of several forms. Sometimes there is the problem of exactly what certain words or phrases meant in the late sixth century B.C.: such doubts, when troublesome, are discussed in Appendix B, the textual notes on the Fragments. Sometimes a modern reader's understanding is hampered by the philosophical, semantic, and grammatical ambiguities discussed above: a difficulty for which there is no secure remedy, but which demands constant alertness of judgment and responsiveness to context. Then again, false scents are sometimes introduced by the later ancient writers who quote the fragments putting their own interpretations upon them. Examples of this difficulty and suggested ways of meeting it are offered and discussed in Appendix B.

Questions both of authenticity and of interpretation have been explored with much industry, scholarship, and ingenuity from the time of Schleiermacher's first compilation of the extant sayings of Heraclitus, in 1817, down to the present day. By general agreement among contemporary scholars the edition of Hermann Diels as revised by Walther Kranz in 1934 is now taken as standard; and the Fragments of Heraclitus that are presented in the following chapters are translated from the Diels-Kranz text, except where otherwise noted in Appendix B. Five Fragments (20, 27, 43, 62, 74) omitted from the Diels-Kranz canon are included here in parentheses, for reasons that Appendix B explains and seeks to justify. The chapters themselves, following the presentation of the Fragments, are meant to be suggestive and per-spectival, not exhaustive or definitive. For the utterances of Heraclitus, like those of the darkly luminous Lord at Delphi (Fr. 18), do not simply speak nor yet simply conceal; they "give signs."

CHAPTER I

THE WAY OF INQUIRY

1. *Although this Logos is eternally valid, yet men are unable to understand it—not only before hearing it, but even after they have heard it for the first time. That is to say, although all things come to pass in accordance with this Logos, men seem to be quite without any experience of it—at least if they are judged in the light of such words and deeds as I am here setting forth. My own method is to distinguish each thing according to its nature, and to specify how it behaves; other men, on the contrary, are as forgetful and heedless in their waking moments of what is going on around and within them as they are during sleep.*

2. *We should let ourselves be guided by what is common to all. Yet, although the Logos is common to all, most men live as if each of them had a private intelligence of his own.*

3. *Men who love wisdom should acquaint themselves with a great many particulars.*

4. *Seekers after gold dig up much earth and find little.*

5. *Let us not make arbitrary conjectures about the greatest matters.*

6. *Much learning does not teach understanding.*

7. *Of those whose discourses I have heard, there is not one who attains to the realization that wisdom stands apart from all else.*

8. *I have searched myself.*

9. *It pertains to all men to know themselves and to be temperate.*

10. *To be temperate is the greatest virtue. Wisdom consists in speaking and acting the truth, giving heed to the nature of things.*

11. *The things of which there can be sight, hearing, and learning—these are what I especially prize.*

12. *Eyes are more accurate witnesses than ears.*

13. Eyes and ears are bad witnesses to men having barbarian souls.

14. One should not act or speak as if he were asleep.

15. The waking have one world in common; sleepers have each a private world of his own.

16. Whatever we see when awake is death; when asleep, dreams.

17. Nature loves to hide.

18. The lord whose oracle is at Delphi neither speaks nor conceals, but gives signs.

19. Unless you expect the unexpected you will never find [truth], for it is hard to discover and hard to attain.

EVERY serious approach to philosophy must begin, whether explicitly or not, with some consideration of method. In certain of the most familiar cases the matter is indicated by indirection. Plato shows what is most essential to his method by the dialogue form in which his philosophy is clothed. Most of Aristotle's treatises reveal his concern for order by beginning with a universal: "All men by nature desire to know" (*Metaphysics*), "In any inquiry that has to do with principles. or causes or elements" (*Physics*), "Every art and every science . . . aims at some good" (*Ethics*). Among philosophers since the Renaissance there has been somewhat more of a disposition to formulate methodological postulates explicitly: in particular, Bacon and Locke on the one hand, Descartes, Spinoza, and Kant on the other, have given deliberate attention to the problem; and in a curiously oblique way even Berkeley's *New Essay towards a Theory of Vision* offers, as a corollary of its optical discoveries, a clue to the method that was to produce the central paradox most associated with the philosopher's name. Heraclitus, too, evidently opened his treatise with an explicit avowal of the method he intended to pursue: for according to the testimony of Sextus Empiricus, Frs. 1 and 2 originally stood, the one at the beginning of the work, the other a short distance further on.[1]

A vexed question has arisen concerning the interpretation to be given to the word λόγος as it appears in the first two Fragments. Granted that the literal meaning is something like "word," is the reference primarily to a transcendental and universal Other who speaks as it were, or primarily to the utterance that Heraclitus himself is making? Although the balance of evidence seems to support the former interpretation, no less an authority than John Burnet has maintained the latter.[2]

The argument for a subjective interpretation of λόγος in Frs. 1 and 2 may be put as follows. From what is known about the practice of heading a treatise in early Greece, it is probable that in lieu of a title Heraclitus would have employed a formula such as: "Heraclitus of Ephesus, son of Blosson, speaks as follows."[3] If he did so, and if we are to interpret Sextus as meaning that Fr. 1 occurred immediately after this conventional opening, then it would seem likely that the word λόγος in Fr. 1 was intended to pick up the idea in the verb "speaks" (λέγει) which preceded it; so that on this ground Burnet would appear to be right in supposing that the word λόγος in the Fragment refers primarily to the discourse of Heraclitus himself.

There is a grave objection, however, to accepting so personal an interpretation of the word. Sextus Empiricus, in quoting the passage, appears to interpret the word as bearing a universal and cosmic significance, for two sentences later he writes: "Heraclitus asserts that the common and divine Logos, by participation in which we become rational, is the criterion of truth."[4] Moreover, in Fr. 118, Heraclitus pointedly distinguishes between the Logos and his own personal speech, when he says: "Listening not to me but to the Logos. . . ." Although Burnet's rendering, "It is wise to hearken, not to me, but to my word . . ." can be defended on grounds that are indicated in the Note to Fr. 118, it nevertheless makes awkward sense, and seems to be a result of trying to remain consistent with the interpretation already

[21]

given to λόγος in Fr. 1. But instead of starting out by deciding how to interpret Fr. 1 and then being obliged to interpret Fr. 118 in so forced a manner, it would be a better procedure to keep both Fragments in mind when trying to discover what either of them means. As a matter of fact, Burnet's argument supporting his interpretation of Fr. 1 is not airtight, for neither of the premises on which it rests is quite certain beyond reasonable doubt. On the one hand, it is not certain how exactly Sextus' phrase, "at the beginning of his treatise," is to be understood. Nor, on the other hand, do we know for sure that the treatise was headed by the usual formula, "Heraclitus speaks thus." Moreover, even if such a heading was actually employed, we cannot know how much of a prophetic connotation the word "speaks" may have carried. To a degree that our secular and colloquial habits of thought can scarcely comprehend, the ancient speaker was apt to regard his speaking not as a personal activity but as a voicing forth of a something greater—of a Logos whose character cannot be given, except haltingly and fragmentarily, in the human utterance. On this basis, then, if Burnet's two premises are accepted, it might still be possible to interpret the opening formula as signifying, "Heraclitus voices forth the Logos as follows"; the reference of "this Logos" in Fr. 1 would thus be to the cosmic principle and not to the personal discourse.

A somewhat analogous interpretation is pertinent to Fr. 2. "Although the Logos is common to all, most men live as if each of them had a private intelligence of his own." Burnet's version, "Although my word is common . . . ," besides lacking any justification in the Greek text, substitutes a confused and queer meaning for the natural one. What can be meant by saying that "my word" is common to all? Whatever meaning it might possess would seem to be at odds with Heraclitus' fiercely aristocratic temper. Once again, the clue for a reasonable interpretation is found in Sextus Empiricus. For after quoting Fr. 1 Sextus writes, "Having in these words argued that we do and think everything through participation in the divine Logos. . . ." Then, after quoting Fr. 2, he goes on to remark: "And this is nothing else than an explanation of the way in which the entirety of things is arranged. Therefore, insofar as we share in the memory of this we say what is true, but when we depend on private experience we say what is false."[5] Editors differ as to whether "this," in the memory of which we may share, refers to "the entirety of things" or to the word "Logos" in the sentence preceding. But in either case it seems clear enough that Sextus understands the word "Logos" as having a cosmic and universal sort of reference.

An interesting light, although no direct evidence, is thrown on the problem by a fragment from a near contemporary of Heraclitus, one Epicharmus of Syracuse, who flourished about 480 to 470 B.C. He was a writer of comedies who occasionally ventured into philosophical speculation, and the following passage from his philosophical writings is quoted by Clement of Alexandria. "The Logos," Epicharmus writes, "steers men and ever preserves them in the right way. Man has the power of calculation, but there is also the divine Logos. Human reasoning is sprung from the divine Logos, which furnishes to each man the passageway of both life and nourishment."[6]

At any rate, as I have remarked in the Introduction, the solution to such questions is not to be found in terms of a sharp either-or. The strongest likelihood is that Heraclitus regarded the Logos as the Truth in its objective and trans-human character, and yet also regarded himself as being especially qualified and privileged to reveal the nature of that truth. To be sure, the word λόγος also means "word," and thus the connotation "what is spoken" attaches to it. But the connoted idea of speaking is largely metaphorical and transcendental; much as when nowadays, with somewhat less conviction, we employ the phrase, "the voice of truth." In Heraclitus' day the sage (σοφός) or lover of wisdom (φιλόσοφος) was still the man who found himself called, by

[23]

the voice of a presence greater than he, to speak forth the truth as it might be revealed to him.

What does Heraclitus mean by describing the truth as "common"? The meaning is put accurately by Kirk and Raven, who write: "The great majority fail to recognize this truth, which is 'common'—that is, both valid for all things and accessible for all men, if only they use their observation and their understanding and do not fabricate a private and deceptive intelligence."[7] The accidental fact that the Greek word for "common," current in Heraclitus' day, and an expression meaning "with mind" sounded so nearly alike as to enable him to connect them in a repeated pun, evidently struck Heraclitus as significant.[8] And although today we are more skeptical of the power of word-magic, we can nevertheless recognize the point of connecting the two meanings. What the pun succeeds in stressing is the natural connection between thinking "with rational awareness" and allowing one's thoughts to be guided by "what is common"—that is, to be guided by the divine Logos which is present in all things and discoverable by all observers if only they will open their eyes and their minds to the fullest possible extent.

These considerations enable us to define with some precision the relation and distinction between Heraclitus' statement of method and the method which may be termed, in a responsible sense of the word, that of mysticism. Although the word "mysticism" is often used loosely and pejoratively, it can be given and should be given a fairly definite sense, with regard both to doctrine and to practice. Mysticism as a philosophy is the doctrine that truth, at least in its higher forms, can be known only by participation in the divine; and the practice of mysticism is the attempt to find ways of realizing such participation. By this definition (which reflects the twin central themes of the most characteristic mystical writings) ought Heraclitus to be described as mystical, or ought he not? There is a limited acceptance of the principle of mysticism in his doctrine that right method involves the kindling of a fiery light of intelligence within one's soul, which is consubstantial with the fiery intelligence that is cosmic activity; or, changing the metaphor, that the only valid knowledge about the greatest matters is that which comes to one who listens to the Logos and attunes his mind to it. Whichever metaphor is employed, that of Light or that of the Word, there is at least an overtone of suggestion that we come to know reality not by merely knowing *about* it (cf. Fr. 6), but by becoming of its nature. One can know the fiery light of intelligence only by becoming a fiery light of intelligence himself; one can hear the divine Word only by becoming an expression of It through voice and deed.

Nevertheless it would be misleading to attach the words "mysticism" and "mystical" to the method of Heraclitus, in view of the many connotations that are popularly attached to them. If, as seems likely, the adjective "mystical" is associated in many people's minds with the adjective "misty," connoting vagueness and intellectual looseness, then nothing could be more opposed to Heraclitus' method and doctrine. If there is any element of mysticism in Heraclitus' conception of the upward way towards light, it is at any rate a mysticism not of sleep but of waking alertness. Heraclitus has nothing in common with the type of mystic who thinks to achieve participation in the divine, and thus to find truth, by going into a trance. In sleep and trance there is nothing but a private world of dreams (Frs. 15, 16); knowledge, on the other hand, can be attained only by becoming vigorously awake, which is to say by employing the faculties of sight, hearing, and learning (Fr. 11) in order to know the facts about the world of which we are part.

Hippolytus quotes Fr. 11 directly after Fr. 116, which declares that the hidden harmony is better than the obvious. Whether or not the two statements were juxtaposed in Heraclitus' original treatise we do not know, but they may well have been so, for they represent two sides of the truth, and it would doubtless have seemed to Heraclitus appro-

priately effective to let them stand in sharp contrast. Hippolytus builds a logical bridge over the antithesis by explaining
that Heraclitus "commends and admires what is unknown
and invisible with respect to its power," but that he holds
what is known to men, and not what is undiscoverable, to be
preferable. These two clauses appear in Hippolytus' *Refutation of All Heresies* between his quotations of Fr. 116 and
Fr. 11. Perhaps they do not go far to explicate the paradox,
but I think the general meaning becomes clear as we reflect
upon them. Heraclitus desires to avoid the kind of misty
mysticism to which his principle of the "identity" (or rather
the coalescence and interplay) of opposites might easily lead
if it were embraced without the necessary qualifications.
Hence he warns us that eyes, ears, and understandings are
the best witnesses; it is preferable to make our souls dry (Fr.
46), and the way to do this is not by falling asleep but by
opening our avenues of perception to the testimonies of
existence as they are offered. But at the same time we should
recognize that any piece of evidence, or any combination of
evidences, is but a small patch of an expanse whose vastness
transcends the powers of human understanding, and that the
harmonies or disharmonies that become manifest to us may
give us a very partial and distorted view of "what is unknown and invisible with respect to its power."

Just as in principle the stress on the value of perceptual
experience is balanced and qualified by a recognition of the
hidden harmony, or secret adjustment, that is effectively at
work in all things, so too as a practical measure one's appeal
to the senses must be fortified by discrimination and self-
discipline. "Eyes and ears are bad witnesses to men having
barbarian souls" (Fr. 13)—that is (as suggested by the
derivation of the Greek adjective), to men who can make
only meaningless sounds like "bar bar," and so cannot com-
municate. Again, the mere accumulation of details is not
enough; polymathy does not teach understanding (Fr. 6).
Although a knowledge of many particulars is important

(Fr. 3), yet it serves a good purpose only so far as one's discovery and interpretation of them are guided by listening to the Logos. Moreover, the outward search must be accompanied by an inner search (Frs. 8, 9), for each self is a microcosm that reflects, in minuscule, the essential nature of reality at large. This is not the closet mysticism of the sleeper, for one's inward discoveries are not to be cut off from one's discoveries of the outer world, which will always provide the surer basis for knowledge and interpretation.

In no important respect is the search for truth easy, nor will its results be obvious. For nature conceals herself beneath vague indications and dark hints (Frs. 17, 18). There is a hidden attunement in nature, the discovery of which is far more deeply rewarding than the mere observation of surface patterns. Everything is interwoven with everything else; nothing stays fixed, and even at a given moment an event or situation can be seen in a number of aspects, some of them representing sharply antithetical and "contradictory" points of view. Such a changing and problematical world cannot be known by easy or static conceptions. There must be an activity and resilience of the mind, corresponding to the ever fluctuating character of the world it seeks to know. Heraclitus, by his own train of reasoning, was moving toward a principle that Pythagoras had taught and that Plato was later to arrive at on the basis of a different philosophy: that truth can be known only by keeping the mind in active athletic trim.

The need for mental athleticism is especially indicated in Frs. 16 and 19. Truth can be found only by "expecting the unexpected"—which is to say, only by an intellectual risk and venturesomeness, a practice of living always on the verge and being ready for whatever vicissitudes may befall. There are no secure mental safety-plays, and to search for them is to seek comforting error instead of truth. The sleeper may enjoy his dreams, including dreams of security and of great things ahead; but the waking man, whose soul is a dancing spurt of flame, knows that there is no security, and that the promises of things to come are as fanciful and uncertain as any of the other dreams in which we are tempted to put our trust. For the future may turn out to be so utterly different from what we had counted on, that it is virtually as if, in the perspective of our present standpoint, there were to be no future for us at all. Whatever we see when awake is changing—which is to say, there is coalescence everywhere and at every moment between some aspects of things dying and some other aspects of things being born and rising to greater power. It is only by looking clearly and boldly into the ever-present fact of universal death—the death of what is familiar and the birth of something alien—that we can escape the net of self-delusion. The only valid method of inquiry is to renounce one's illusions of permanence and to throw one's lot unreservedly in with the vagaries of the changing world.

CHAPTER II

UNIVERSAL FLUX

*(20. Everything flows and nothing abides; everything gives
way and nothing stays fixed.)*

*21. You cannot step twice into the same river, for other waters
are continually flowing on.*

*22. Cool things become warm, the warm grows cool; the
moist dries, the parched becomes moist.*

23. It is in changing that things find repose.

*24. Time is a child moving counters in a game; the royal
power is a child's.*

*25. War is both father and king of all; some he has shown
forth as gods and others as men, some he has made slaves
and others free.*

*26. It should be understood that war is the common condi-
tion, that strife is justice, and that all things come to pass
through the compulsion of strife.*

*(27. Homer was wrong in saying, "Would that strife might
perish from amongst gods and men." For if that were to
occur, then all things would cease to exist.)*

THE theme of unceasing change is a very old one in philosophy. In every experience and in our normal ways of respond-
ing to that experience it would seem that the proposition,
"Everything changes," represents only a half-truth, although
a very important one. For along with its multifariously shifting, fading, and vanishing aspects the world shows also some
indications of the stable and permanent. Men may come and
men may go, but the truth of the multiplication table does not
budge. Or if that example is rejected as a mere conceptual
abstraction, one can point to certain more substantial fixities
within the physical environment itself. Although the houses
may all go under the hill, Mother Earth remains solidly herself; although individuals and societies sprout and fall like

leaves, the human race somehow goes on. Or even, as a precarious corollary of the thermonuclear age, if we should at last succeed in blowing up the earth and exterminating mankind, presumably the stars would continue on their orbits, majestically unmoved by our mundane fidgetings. What experience and imagination jointly offer to our view, it would seem, is the changing and the permanent in varying combinations.

The philosophy of change as represented by Heraclitus goes a step further however. Permanence is but a relative term, his philosophy declares; and what we call permanent is simply an example of change in slow motion or in hidden guise. All structures, if you observe them patiently enough and project your imagination far enough, are dissolving slowly; everything, as the Greeks put it, is in process of coming-to-be and passing-away.[1] Obviously when Heraclitus says that everything flows and gives way, he does not mean that everything does so at the same rate or with the same degree of outward apparency. To our daily life of sensation and impulse it makes a great deal of difference whether something lasts five seconds or five weeks or five billion years, but such differences do not affect the underlying principle that sooner or later each thing must come to an end. The time-spans of a lightning flash, of a human career, and of the course of evolution from protozoon to man, are all finite time-spans despite their obviously different lengths: that is the self-evident truth on which the philosophy of change hinges. Moreover, even in what appears to be most solid and perduring there is some change going on all the while; even where no evidence of change is visible to the eye, the presumption is that everything is undergoing some secret alteration in one way or another at every moment. To Heraclitus' concretely philosophical imagination this universal condition is symbolically represented by the flowing river, in which you cannot step twice, and by fire the most volatile of all physical things.

When Heraclitus says that everything is undergoing some

degree of alteration at every moment, he must be understood in his own context and not in ours. A literate person today would readily admit, if he stopped to think about the matter, that the apparently solid and inert table on which he rests his elbow "is really" a collection of rapidly moving molecules, and that the visible color of the table "is really" a mental and subjective impression brought about by vibrations of a certain frequency striking the optical nerves. Heraclitus knew nothing about all this, and hence he certainly could not be referring to it. In saying that everything is constantly changing, what he refers to is a phenomenon much closer to actual experience than the scientific doctrine of molecular movement is for most of us. The meaning can be discovered by a simple test. Try staring at some colorful object long enough, and if your perceptual memory is keen you will find that some change has come into the visible quality during the long process of staring at it. The blue of the sky is likely to become a somewhat duller blue after too prolonged a gazing. Similarly with the kinds of qualities presented by hearing, taste, and touch. To such observations the modern reply is likely to be that what has changed is not the thing itself but merely our perception of it. But it must be remembered that this psychophysical dualism, which for the past three centuries or so has been an *idée fixe* with most of us, was not a natural and required starting-point for thinking in Heraclitus' day. For him, as for most Greek thinkers, qualities are in the main what they appear to be; they are properties of things primarily, of minds secondarily; and the distinction between the thing beheld and the mind beholding it was loose and fluctuating. Heraclitus was one who looked at the world with the eye of a painter, or of a child; and his powerful speculations about the nature of things were reared upon that basis. In the qualitative sense all things are constantly changing because the qualities themselves are wavering, and for Heraclitus a thing is nothing more than the complete set of all the qualities and powers that belong to and constitute it.

Examining the concept of qualitative change more closely we may discover two main ways in which it is natural to conceive of such change as occurring: either as a passage from some quality to its opposite or else as a passage from one stage to another of a serial order. Both these extensions of the idea played an important role in the development of Greek philosophy and science. There are some changes that do not readily and immediately lend themselves to either of the two types of schematism: for instance, the purely qualitative change of, say, the sky from blue to pink at sunset. Blue and pink are not opposites in any usual sense of the word. Nor do they fall into an immediately evident series in the way that different shades of blue, or different shades of pink and red, might do. To be sure, when the colors are seen in a rainbow or in a photometer they do then occupy definite places in the spectrum, and thereby in that context they possess a serial character; in ordinary contexts, however, they do not. The concept of series, in one form or another, has been of the greatest importance in the development of science—a development that finds its starting-point, so far as historical evidence reveals, in the early cosmology of Anaximenes. Heraclitus gives recognition to the serial concept in his various references to the upward and downward ways—in Frs. 32, 34, 46-49, and more lightly in several other Fragments. But on the whole his conception of change is governed by the first of the two schemes. Change is an alteration from opposite to opposite: whereas it was cool it is now warm, and whereas it was humid it is now dry (Fr. 22). There is a sense, indeed, in which such a way of conceiving change is inescapable: a color change can be considered as an alteration from lighter to darker or the reverse, or from prettier to uglier or the reverse; the passage from winter to summer can be described as the cold turning into warmth; and even locomotion, when given a personal reference, can be regarded in terms of something losing its hereness and taking on the opposite character of thereness. Such ways of thinking and speaking seem strange to us because we have largely lost the radically humanistic perspective, which the Greeks still retained, and wherein the first step in wisdom (not the last, but always the first!) is to describe each thing not as we think we know it to be, but as it directly appears to an actively percipient mind.

Nevertheless, even if we are concerned with change in its directly perceived character—which is to say, as an alteration of quality, not as a conceptualized movement of molecules—it is still an odd thing for us, and a violation of our linguistic and intellectual habits, to speak of the warm becoming cool, the moist becoming dry, and so on. We can see what the trouble is by a very simple mental and linguistic experiment. Instead of saying, "The warm becomes cool" or "The warm becomes the cool," let us try the experiment of saying, "What was warm becomes cool." Presto, the oddity and the sense of paradox have disappeared. We are no longer burdened with the troublesome idea of something turning into its own opposite; we have substituted for that paradox the more manageable idea of an unspecified something, a "what," which can successively wear the attributes of warm and cool in somewhat the same way in which a person might successively wear different suits of clothes. In forming a conception of change we find ourselves constrained to think, as Aristotle has demonstrated, not dyadically in terms of two opposites alone, but triadically in terms of the pair of opposites and a substance or substratum or subject or thing in which the opposites are conceived successively to inhere. "It is hard to conceive," Aristotle remarks, "how density and rarity, for instance, each retaining its essential nature, could in any way act upon each other."[2] Consequently, he concludes, "we must postulate the existence of a third something" that is logically distinct from the pair of opposite qualities which successively inhere in it. Sometimes the third something has a name denoting a set of recognizable qualities other than the opposites in question. Thus, when hot soup cools or when thin soup thickens—omitting all reference to physical theories about heat and evaporation, which are known to the average person by hearsay, or at best by indirect experiment and ratiocination—we fall quite spontaneously into the triadic way of thinking, for the meaning of "soup" is familiar to us through other properties, and we can easily think of hot and cold, thin and thick, as qualities that are distinct from the soup itself. But there are other situations, other forms of experience, where there is no specific subject already within purview and we have to invent one by a linguistic maneuver. Thus, when in ordinary conversation someone remarks, "It was cool, but now it has become warm," what do we take the word "it" to refer to? If challenged on the point a person might perhaps retort, "the weather"; but obviously the new word tells nothing more than the word "it" had done. Neither "it" nor "the weather" gives us any knowledge that would not have been already contained in the Heraclitean statement, "Cool has become warm," or "The cool has become the warm." The difference is not empirical, it is syntactical and epistemological. The preferred linguistic convention expresses a conceptual need. Most persons are uneasy in contemplating change in so radical a manner as Heraclitus does; they require, as a conceptual-prop, the idea of "something, I know not what" underlying the changing particulars. In this respect, although perhaps without knowing it, they are Aristotelians.

Heraclitus, on the contrary, is not an Aristotelian: neither grammatically nor conceptually does he share Aristotle's need for "a third something that endures" in any alteration from opposite to opposite. To him every change is a knock-down battle between two ontological opposites, and there is no referee—neither a Platonic higher Form nor an Aristotelian "underlying substance"—that can be regarded as standing logically outside the process. Even deity is no exception. Particular gods and demigods, although superior to men (Frs. 104, 105), are finite and will eventually be transformed from gods into something else (Fr. 66). On the other hand, a

divine name when employed in a comprehensive and absolute
sense stands for the total self-organizing and self-destroying
process itself; as when Heraclitus is said to declare (although
we do not possess a direct quotation on this point) that *war
and Zeus are the same thing*.[3] Since conflict is the ultimate
condition of everything, it alone merits the epithets of divinity. What is ultimate must be conceived as strife, war, and
tension; peace and stability are either strife in slow motion or
at most a temporary lull between one flare-up of strife and
another.

If strife is fundamental, then it follows that humanly significant results come about not from any planning but by
chance. Conditions may at one time be propitious to life, or
even to the higher forms of life and thought; at another time
they may be destructive and annihilating. When conscious
life beholds a set of conditions that have been favorable to its
development, it tends to regard such conditions as produced
by a cosmic purpose that is somehow concerned with the
welfare and destiny of such living forms as its own. Heraclitus
rejects any such assumption as unwarranted. If we are going
to employ a human analogy in speaking of the guiding of the
universe as a whole, let us describe it not as a mature, wise,
and kindly God, but rather as an irresponsible child idly
moving counters in a game (Fr. 24).

But if chance is characteristic of universal process, what is
to be made of the statement, which Stobaeus ascribes to Heraclitus, that all things occur as they are destined? To be sure,
Diels omits the fragment from his list, but Bywater accepts
it, and my point is that even if it is authentic—even if, indeed,
the ensuing remark in Stobaeus that "the destiny has the
character of necessity" is to be taken as part of the quotation from Heraclitus,[4]—still there is no real difficulty about
reconciling it with the doctrine that things happen by chance.
The ideas of chance and necessity are not mutually contradictory but, as Aristotle has shown,[5] they represent the non-
human aspect of things in two different perspectives. From

the humanistic point of view, whatever lies outside the range of human planning can be said to happen "by chance" so far as human purposes are concerned; and the Greeks expressed the unhumanistic nature of such events by applying to them the metallic word ἀνάγκη, "necessity." A necessary event is so described not because some cosmic tyrant pushes it into being, but precisely because no one does so. Therefore, from the standpoint of anyone whom it affects, the event may be described as fortuitous, accidental, something that has happened "by chance." To say that the universe flows along as it is destined, or by necessity, and to say that "the royal power is a child's," or that the counters are moved arbitrarily and by chance, are different ways of asserting that the major occurrences in the universe lie outside the range and power of any man or god; they run along by themselves, as a result of many forces, which are most characteristically in conflict, but which sometimes enter into temporary and limited alliances, and which somehow manage in their fluctuations to reveal glimpses of a subtle and largely hidden harmony.

CHAPTER III

THE PROCESSES OF NATURE

28. There is exchange of all things for fire and of fire for all things, as there is of wares for gold and of gold for wares.

29. This universe, which is the same for all, has not been made by any god or man, but it always has been, is, and will be —an ever-living fire, kindling itself by regular measures and going out by regular measures.

30. [The phases of fire are] craving and satiety.

31. It throws apart and then brings together again; it advances and retires.

32. The transformations of fire are: first, sea; and of sea, half becomes earth, and half the lightning-flash.

33. When earth has melted into sea, the resultant amount is the same as there had been before the sea became hardened into earth.

34. Fire lives in the death of earth, air in the death of fire, water in the death of air, and earth in the death of water.

35. The thunderbolt pilots all things.

36. The sun is new each day.

37. The sun is the breadth of a man's foot.

38. If there were no sun, the other stars would not suffice to prevent its being night.

39. The boundary line of evening and morning is the Bear; and opposite the Bear is the boundary of bright Zeus.

40. The fairest universe is but a heap of rubbish piled up at random.

41. Every beast is driven to pasture by a blow.

HERACLITUS' principle of a continually changing universe—what Spengler calls the "first formulation" of his theory[1]—is symbolized not only by such diverse figures as the flowing river and the child idly moving counters in a game, but also and most centrally, by fire. Fire is the most significant of the several symbols by which the Heraclitean idea of change is expressed: first, because it has not just one basis of symbolic connection with the central idea, but at least three; and secondly, because Heraclitus regards fire as playing not only a symbolic but also a literal role of importance in his doctrine of the cosmos. The three main properties of fire that give it so important a symbolic role are its light and brightness, its warmth and consequent ability to effect changes such as in cooking, and its unique agility and power of rapid self-increase. The clear glow of wisdom in which outlines and distinctions are made visible, the enthusiasm and urgency to create, and the quickness and alertness of mind and spirit, which these properties respectively tend to symbolize, are what have given to fire (in its broadest sense, including the sun and the sparkle of daylight in the upper air) its perennial symbolic importance. These meanings are present in Heraclitus' thinking too, but as is quite generally the case with ancient thinkers he did not distinguish between vehicle and tenor sharply, and it is evident that he thinks of fire not only as meaning something other than itself, but also as a physical thing (albeit a fast moving and elusive thing) playing a definite role in the natural world. Spengler's often brilliant study of Heraclitus is sometimes marred by his overemphasis upon the symbolic role of fire, as connoting the idea of pure occurrence. Spengler is right in declaring that for Heraclitus the most basic ontological fact is the ongoingness of things, and their unceasing alteration from one manifestation to another. But so far as he indulges his own zest for rational clarity by clearly formulating the idea of pure change, and then supposing that Heraclitus employed the image of fire as a symbol for this pure idea—so far as he does this, he is oversimplifying. Any pure scientific and philosophical idea such as that of abstract change is of later development, and it is an anachronism to attribute it to Heraclitus. Philosophical ideas as they were formulated by the thinkers of the sixth century

B.C.—even by the greatest of them—were rather like those statues of Rodin in which some part of a living figure, usually the head and torso, is carved into clear and significant shape, but where the shaped portions seem to be a living and incomplete outgrowth from the mass of unhewn stone below. Heraclitus, like the Milesian philosophers before him, was making a great contribution to the clarification of physical process; but the intellectual sculpturing was not yet complete, and a modern critic errs and distorts if he insists upon finding clarity to a greater degree than it exists. A historian of ideas must develop his "negative capability," picking up the traces of form where he finds them but without pretending that the formal elements of an ancient doctrine can be set forth in totally clear outline according to present-day categories.

As opposed to those who overstress the symbolic role of fire in Heraclitus, there are scholars such as Teichmüller who treat fire as merely a physical actuality, ignoring or denying or belittling its symbolic role.[2] According to this standpoint, Heraclitus is doing in the main the same thing that the Milesian physicists had done before him—seeking in one of the recognized elements of nature (traditionally taken to be fire, air, water, and earth) for a basic cause and first principle upon which a structure of physical science could be built. Teichmüller argues (very reasonably, so far as the physical aspect of fire is concerned) that Heraclitus' ground for choosing this substance in preference to the water of Thales or the air of Anaximenes was his perception that it is the purest and noblest substance, having its natural residence in the upper sky, where there is no moisture, and where the sun can be a clear unadulterated fiery light.

The emphasis upon a physical interpretation of the Heraclitean fire stems from ancient times. So far as our extant documentary evidence can tell, it was Aristotle and some of his commentators, along with several writers in the doxographical tradition stemming from Theophrastus, who gave ancient currency to the idea. Thus in *De Caelo* Aristotle speaks of those who explain the universe by reference to a single basic element—a remark which he specifies by adding that some take the basic element to be water, others air, others fire, and others something midway between water and air.[3] Although Heraclitus is not here mentioned by name, the reference is clearly to him and his followers, and the main thought to be noticed is that Aristotle is taking the theory of fire as parallel to the theories of water and air. Similarly in the *Metaphysics*, after speaking of the view of Anaximenes that air is "most truly the first principle (ἀρχή) of all simple bodies," he mentions by way of contrast the view of Heraclitus that such a role is played by fire.[4] Quite naturally Aristotle's commentators usually fall into line with this interpretation. Asclepius contrasts Heraclitus' doctrine of fire as the first principle with Thales' doctrine of water and Anaximander's doctrine of air. All three of the elements he takes as "material causes" of things. The commentators Alexander Aphrodisiensis and Simplicius say virtually the same thing.[5]

Now, as has been remarked in the Introduction, in interpreting Heraclitus it is necessary to bracket off our modern ways of thinking and enter into his own, and one of the respects in which this can be done is by a readiness to think in terms of *both-and*, not merely of *either-or*. Heraclitus' fire is at once the material element, the familiar flame that burns and crackles, and yet, too, it is the embodiment and symbol of change in general.[6] But even this double aspect does not exhaust its nature. For fire is also known as the inner light of intelligence and spiritual awareness—a light that is at the same time a warm but self-disciplined activity; and since Heraclitus does not think of a sharp demarcation between the inner world of self-knowledge and the outer world of nature, it follows that he thinks of fire as somehow endowed with intelligence. In acknowledging that characteristic we must avoid, if we would interpret Heraclitus faithfully, the temptation to personalize fire more completely; to do that would be the way of mythology, which Heraclitus, following his fellow-Ionian Xenophanes, repudiates. Nevertheless, it is clear that he does think of fire not merely as a principle of transformation and as an element in the transformation (ideas that are variously expressed and intermingled in Frs. 28, 29, 32, and 34) but also as somehow directing and piloting all things. In Fr. 35 it is a special manifestation of fire in the sky, and a very audible one— the thunderclap, usually accompanied or preceded by a lightning flash—that is said to "pilot" all things. In Fr. 120, where the idea of piloting is expressed by a different but synonymous Greek verb, the guiding power is described as "intelligence." Comparison of Frs. 35 and 120 strongly suggests that the ideas of fire and intelligence were, to Heraclitus' mind, interchangeable or at any rate closely related and mutually coalescent. In addition, there are passages in the doxographers which show that there was a generally held later opinion that Heraclitus had made such a coupling. For instance, Hippolytus, in introducing Fr. 30, declares that for Heraclitus "fire is characterized by intelligence, and is responsible for the management of the universe"; while Stobaeus offers the intriguing statement, "Heraclitus held that the cosmos is generated not by time but by mind."[7]

Concerning the physical aspect of fire it is important to think of it in ancient, not modern terms. The tendency of modern physics, roughly since Galileo,[8] has been to reënvisage all kinds of change as caused by, and as epiphenomena of, movements in space (what Aristotle calls "locomotions"), and to regard the moving parts of a thing, which we cannot see, as more real than the perceptible and tangible characteristics. This was not the Greek way of viewing the matter, and it was not Heraclitus' way. When he speaks of a process of continual change, he refers to an observable process of changing qualities of the thing as a whole, and not to the changing locations of its minuscule parts. However, it must be admitted that ancient Greece, too, had its speculative reductionists, although their characteristic ways of reducing

were different from ours. The so-called atomism of Leucippus and Democritus (roughly what we mean by the molecular theory, if the molecules could be thought of as not being
further divisible into atomic parts) was but one speculative
theory among others. A hint of another and more curious
sort of theory is furnished by Simplicius' remark that fire
as Heraclitus conceived it is irreducibly fire and is "not composed of pyramids."[9] Evidently there must have been a theory
abroad in ancient Greece that fire did consist, or might consist, of pyramids. Aristotle, who regards the theory as rather
quaint and implausible, mentions two reasons for it. On the
one hand the pyramid is the most piercing of solid figures,
as fire is the most piercing of physical elements—a crude
argument, Aristotle observes. On the other hand, the pyramid (evidently he means one with a triangular base, which
is to say a tetrahedron) is the simplest of solid figures, and
therefore by ancient logic could be regarded as an element
in all other solid figures. Simplicius, in commenting upon
this passage in Aristotle, declares firmly that Heraclitus regarded fire as the basic, irreducible element in all things and
did not think of it as composed of pyramids—nor, it may
be added, as composed of any other geometrical form nor
of any set of locomotions.

Fire, then—ignoring for the moment its further symbolic
meanings—is fire as seen and felt, the familiar qualitative
entity with which everyone is acquainted; but it must be
added that the brightness, warmth, and activity of fire are
both outward and inward at once, for there is not yet any
clear division between chemistry and psychology. Regarding
fire in this way (and not as "composed of pyramids") we
cannot, of course, conceive of change as molecular or atomic
movement.

How, then, is change to be conceived? The end of Fr. 29
gives the most natural answer in terms of the dominant
imagery: the cosmic fire becomes "kindled" and "extinguished"—both processes taking place "by regular meas-

ures." Evidently this is a more definitely physical way of conceiving what Heraclitus calls in Fr. 108 the upward and downward ways. The double process, on its physical side, is described more specifically in Fr. 32. Fire is here said to transform itself into two other types of manifestation— sea and earth, representing with fire the three main stages of physical transformation. But in the return passage upwards the earth turns again into sea, and the sea, or part of it, turns into fire, which is now more dramatically and concretely spoken of as the lightning flash ($\pi\rho\eta\sigma\tau\acute{\eta}\rho$).

It is impossible to find an English word that accurately translates $\pi\rho\eta\sigma\tau\acute{\eta}\rho$, for the plain reason that the meteorological phenomenon to which the Greek word refers is not found in English-speaking countries. There has been a good deal of dispute, among both ancient and modern writers, as to just what the phenomenon is. Epicurus, in a passage in his letter to Pythocles, seems to describe it as a kind of whirlwind or cyclone accompanied by a water-spout. Later, Lucretius speaks in his poem of "what the Greeks have called $\pi\rho\eta\sigma\tau\acute{\eta}\rho\epsilon\varsigma$," and describes them as "bursting down from above into the sea." In other words, as nearly as I can interpret these two passages, Epicurus thinks of the phenomenon as mainly involving an upward motion ("water-spout") and Lucretius as mainly involving a downward. Neither of the passages directly mentions its fiery character; but Cyril Bailey, in commenting upon the latter passage, interprets the Greek word as implying the presence of fire. Whether his etymology is accepted or not, there is a confirmatory statement by Seneca, who, writing on types of wind, says that what the Greeks called $\pi\rho\eta\sigma\tau\acute{\eta}\rho$ is something that bursts into flame (*inflammatur*) and is a fiery whirl (*igneus turbo*). Moreover, some kind of ignition is evidently implied by Aëtius' statement that the phenomenon is caused "by the kindling and extinction of clouds."[10] Consequently, although there is some doubt as to precise descriptive details, one main fact about the phenomenon is clear: that it is a meteorological occurrence which in some manner combines water, wind, and fire in its composition, and hence it serves Heraclitus as a vivid and appropriate exhibition of the physical interchange that goes on naturally between water and fire, although more prominently at some times and places than at others.

One further remark by Lucretius may throw an incidental light upon Heraclitus' view of how the elements interrelate. He states that a πρηστήρ rarely spends its force over the land, where the hills would tend to break it up, but more often over the sea "with its wide prospect and open sky." This remark may be compared with Heraclitus' view of the sea as playing the role of intermediary between the passive earth and the violently active πρηστήρ.

But how is the lightning flash of Fr. 32 related to the thunderbolt of Fr. 35? They are certainly not to be distinguished as the ideas of lightning and thunder are distinguished in our modern languages, which take the one as visible, the other as audible. From the various instances of both words in Greek literature it is clear that both a visual and an auditory meaning are attached to each of them. Perhaps the first word puts a slightly greater emphasis upon the visual properties while the second puts a slightly greater emphasis upon the auditory properties, but the two sets of properties cannot be separated; for, whichever word was employed in a given case, the Greeks tended to think in terms of the whole phenomenon, visual and auditory aspects combined. Thus Kirk is probably right in remarking that the thunderbolt (Fr. 35) "may stand as a name for fire in general, or perhaps for celestial fire in particular."[11] Both words furnish instances of ontological synecdoche; each of them offers a particular sort of observable phenomenon, at once fiery and dramatically impressive (probably tonal too), as an "eminent instance" (to use Goethe's phrase) of the universal fiery quasi-intelligence that steers all things through all things (Fr. 120).

Now the ideas of kindling and extinguishing, as employed in modern Western language and thought, apply only to the uppermost phase of the cosmic process—the passage of other forms of matter into and out of fire. While it is not certain whether the words for "kindling" and "extinguishing," as quoted by Clement in Fr. 29, were employed by Heraclitus for the lower, subaqueous phases of the process, the fact remains that, whatever word or words he may have used, Heraclitus evidently thought of the upper and lower phases of the process as mutually continuous and hence as graspable in terms of a single concept. In Fr. 33 he speaks of earth as "melting" into sea, and of sea as "hardening" into earth. In several doxographical references to Heraclitus, on the other hand, it is not "melting" but rather "evaporation" that describes the passage from earth into something more fluid. Even if the Greek word for "evaporation" which is found in later writers (ἀναθυμίασις) is of later coinage, some idea of the evaporative process must of course have been familiar at a much earlier period. There is a passage in Aëtius which suggests that it may have been Thales who first put scientific stress upon the idea of evaporation in natural process. Plutarch, in his version of the same passage, is evidently speaking with careful accuracy, for he numbers his points. The third doctrine that he here attributes to Thales is "that even the very fire of the sun and stars, and indeed the cosmos itself, is nourished by evaporation of the waters."[12] I can see no reason for doubting Plutarch's statement that Thales held such a view; for surely it is reasonable enough that Thales, starting with the postulate that the basic substance is water, should have conceived of evaporation as the primary process of nature. If he did so, then the idea of evaporation may well have been carried on in the Milesian school as an important scientific concept. The sparseness of documentary evidence prevents our knowing what word or words may have been employed to express the concept, but I would think it probable that some word was in use—although perhaps not the "efflux" that was questionably attributed to Anaximenes[13]—a word broad enough, or semantically flexible enough, to combine into one concept the ideas of melting, evaporation, and perhaps even of bursting into flame. It may be, too, that in referring to the contrary physical process, from fire downward to earth, the early Milesian scientists employed a similarly broad and flexible concept to include the ideas of self-extinguishing (applied to fire as it becomes transformed into something grosser), liquefying (from an airy to an aqueous state), and solidifying. The hypothesis is doubtless speculative, but it is not without some degree of scattered evidence. Now if the ideas of evaporation and condensation, in the broad sense here indicated, were current in sixth century Miletus, it is not at all improbable that by the end of the century Heraclitus, living some twenty-five miles away, would have become acquainted with them; nor is it improbable that, despite his vaunted independence of other thinkers, he might have been influenced by them. Even the most original of thinkers reaches out sometimes for other men's conceptual structures, which he may then adapt to his own ideas; and it may well be that Heraclitus was more indebted to certain Milesian ways of thinking than he realized. (It is to be noted that, although he hurls some scathing words against Homer, Hesiod, and Pythagoras, there is no record of his having made any derogatory allusion to the scientists of the neighboring city of Miletus.) The notion which he seems most likely to have taken from the Milesian school of thought, and then to have adapted and varied according to the demands of his own more active imagination, is that of the double physical process which might be loosely indicated by the words rarefaction and condensation. Since Heraclitus was above all a perspectival thinker, always ready and alert to readapt his viewpoint to the changing character of whatever might confront him, and to the variously seen many-sidedness of every phenomenon, he would have recognized as different guises of much the same thing the upward way, the process of thinning, the two-phased process of evaporation and conflagration, and (inwardly) the struggle toward intellectual integrity and self-knowledge.

But now comes a question over which there has been much scholarly dispute. Do the upward and downward processes of nature involve three main stages or four? Fr. 32 indicates the former alternative, Fr. 34 the latter. Is air, which is mentioned in Fr. 34 and not in Fr. 32, a real stage in the Heraclitean cosmology, or is it not? Certain scholars have gone so far as to deny the authenticity of Fr. 34, or to regard it as a mangled version of what Heraclitus really said.[14] Now it is possible, to be sure, that Maximus of Tyre, who quotes the Fragment as it stands and who is a genial but not always exact thinker, may have taken from Heraclitus simply the general idea of the physical elements living and dying in relation to one another, and in formulating it may have spoken loosely in terms of the more familiar doctrine of the elements as fourfold, ignoring Heraclitus' threefold scheme as being irrelevant to his purpose as a moralizing essayist. But on the other hand there is the somewhat confirmatory version of the quotation as given by Plutarch: "The death of fire is the birth of air, the death of air is the birth of water."[15] Although earth is ignored in the statement, the three elements that are mentioned include air, which is the distinctive element in Fr. 34 and is omitted from Fr. 32.

Assuming, then, that the Fragment is quoted correctly, a possible explanation of the discrepancy might be that Heraclitus held the two views at different stages of his philosophical career—i.e., that he began by accepting the conventional notion of the four elements (fire, air, water, earth) and that he later simplified this conventional schema by leaving out air. A reason for such simplification might be suggested by Fr. 36, for in declaring that a new sun is born and dies each day Heraclitus meant, as Galenus explains, that the sun is moulded each morning out of the waters surrounding the earth and becomes one with the waters again when it drops back into them in the evening.[16] The passage from water to fire and from fire to water is here conceived as direct, without the intermediate state of air having to be assumed.

Another possible hypothesis is that Heraclitus may have held the threefold and the fourfold principles simultaneously, identifying air with soul and hence with what would later be called potentiality, while conceiving the three other elements as actualities. (I grant that Heraclitus possessed no proper words for this Aristotelian pair of ideas, but it is a mark of his genius that he is repeatedly reaching beyond the available vocabulary in an effort to fashion and grasp ideas that he can only haltingly express.) Although such a hypothesis interprets Heraclitus as giving greater prominence to air in his cosmology than he is usually supposed to do, it should not be dismissed without considering one small piece of evidence in its favor. Sextus Empiricus twice mentions an opinion, held by Aenesidemus and others, that Heraclitus took the basic existent to be air. In one passage, speaking of theories about "the primary and fundamental elements," he says that according to some interpretations Heraclitus supposed such elements to be of the nature of air, but that according to others he supposed them to be fire. In the other passage, speaking of "the existent" ($\tau\grave{o}$ $\ddot{o}\nu$), he cites Aenesidemus as saying that Heraclitus considered it to be air.[17] Nothing further is said on the subject, and it must be admitted that no firm conclusion can be drawn from such sparse evidence. Nevertheless, considering that in early Greek times the soul is closely associated with air, and that for Heraclitus soul is the first principle (Fr. 43), considering also the problem of reconciling Frs. 32 and 34, and considering finally that while soul is superior to water (Frs. 44, 49) yet from the general evidence of the Fragments of Chapter IV it is not ordinarily equivalent to pure fire—I would think that at least the hypothesis might be entertained that Heraclitus may have regarded the soul as somehow hovering between the condition of water and that of fire, and therefore as being (according to the natural context of early Greek ontology) something rather like air. Such airiness would be conceived as an unstable and potential state, from which soul could either slip downward into mud or strive upward to the condition of fire.

Two Fragments of the present group, Frs. 30 and 33, suggest dim analogies to certain more developed modern philosophies. In Fr. 33, which can be discussed the more briefly of the two, Heraclitus appears to be groping for a way of stating something like the law of physical conservation. Although his apprehension of the law is of course relatively primitive and vague as compared with the exact formulation it has received in modern physics, nevertheless there is evidently in the Fragment a new insight, an insistence that in the complicated process of physical transformations there is nothing quantitatively either gained or lost; and this represents an important step in the development of scientific thought.

Fr. 30 ("The phases of fire are craving and satiety") is of interest as representing what may be called the empathetic trend in philosophy—the tendency to interpret the essence of outer things and activities in the light of characteristics that we inwardly discover as belonging to ourselves. Physical events, when looked at in anthropocentric perspective, appear to be motivated in a manner somehow similar to our own behavior. But in what terms is that similarity to be expressed? Nietzsche, Schopenhauer, and von Hartmann have spoken in various ways of the *will* in nature; Bergson of the *élan vital* that is at the heart of all activity; others have spoken of *mind* in nature, and the like. But a single word is likely to say too little, or too much, or both too little and too much in different ways. The pair of terms, *craving* and *satiety*, gives appropriate contour to the scarcely sayable notion. Motive power as we know it in nature (storms, plant growth, and animal instincts, as distinguished from the me-

chanical activities of man-made machines) is not homogene-
ous; it does not express itself equally at all times; there are
periods of craving, need, and struggle, and there are periods
of satiety and rest. The opposites are of course polar, temporary, and mutually relative, but they are nonetheless real
and effective aspects of nature as it can be observed.

One of the most disputed questions concerning Heraclitus'
cosmology has to do with whether or not he believed in
world-cycles, and more specifically in the doctrine of ἐκπύρωσις. This word, as used by Stoic writers, designates
the dissolution of the universe by fire. The Stoic doctrine
goes on to say that such dissolution is periodic, occurring
after very long intervals of time, and being eventually followed by the gradual emergence of a new universe out of
the fiery mass. The long period of time between one conflagration and the next, or perhaps between the first appearance
of things out of the cosmic fire and their ultimate extinction
by reabsorption into it, was identified by Stoics with the
ancient doctrine, probably of Chaldaean origin, of the Great
Year. Among the Chaldaeans, who were devoted astrono-
mers and astrologers, the length of such a cosmic period
was believed to be determined by the time it took the seven
known planets (including sun and moon) to come again
into conjunction. In the Chaldaean tradition the length of
the Great Year was taken as equivalent to 36,000 ordinary
years—a figure evidently chosen on some ground other than
exact astronomical computation. Traces of a vaguely similar
doctrine can be found in the literatures of ancient India and
Iran, as well as among some of the cryptic records of the
ancient Mayas and Aztecs. In the Chaldaean doctrine it was
further held that when the conjunction of the planets takes
place in Cancer all things are reduced to water, and that
when it occurs in Capricorn all things become one with, or
are consumed by, fire.[18] Among the Greeks, on the other
hand, the period of the Great Year was usually estimated
as lasting either 18,000 or 10,800 years. The latter figure

held a special appeal to a people eager to find relations between microcosm and macrocosm; for it represents the product of 30 (the average span between one human generation and the next) multiplied by 360 (the formalized notion of the number of days in a year); hence, to the ancient mind, a Great Year of this length would represent a year of human generations, with the span between one generation and the next counting as a day.

Did Heraclitus himself believe in the dissolution of the universe by fire? Among ancient writers, for the most part, it appears to have been supposed that he did. Admittedly the Fragments that are accepted as direct quotations from Heraclitus offer no proof either way. Although the group of Fragments 28 to 34 and Fr. 72 can be interpreted as referring to such a cataclysm if Heraclitus' belief in it could be established on other grounds, they do not prove anything by themselves in this respect, inasmuch as they can all be reasonably interpreted without reference to the doctrine. Each of them might perhaps be describing some aspect of the day-to-day behavior of fire in its relation to the ceaselessly changing world, and without any supposition of a time when fire will consume everything else completely. The question whether Heraclitus did or did not hold the doctrine of world conflagration and world cycles cannot be answered on the evidence of the canonical Fragments alone; most of the evidence, pro and con, must be circumstantial and based on indirect testimony.

The strongest argument against the supposition that Heraclitus believed in such a doctrine has been drawn up by Kirk, on the following counts. He argues (1) that the entire tenor of Heraclitus' argument is against the doctrine, since "the unity of opposites upon which the Logos is founded depends upon the balance between them"; (2) that the doctrine would contradict the emphasis upon "measures" (as in Fr. 29) and upon the "exchange" that goes on between fire and all things (Fr. 28); (3) that it would contradict the statement (Fr. 29) that the universal process "is eternal and will never be destroyed" (Kirk's paraphrase of "always has been, is, and will be"); (4) that it would mean that Plato was grossly mistaken in distinguishing between Empedocles' view that cosmic unity and plurality exist in alternation and Heraclitus' view that the two states exist simultaneously; (5) that "even among Stoic sympathizers there were some who doubted the ἐκπύρωσις-interpretation"; and that the Fragments which are commonly supposed to support the view are of no evidential value for the purpose.[19] The array of arguments is formidable, both by their cumulative force and because of the deserved scholarly reputation of their proponent. They fall short, however, of being conclusive; and in order to be able to consider fairly what can be said on the opposite side of the question I shall briefly examine them one by one.

(1). The first argument seems to me the strongest. Kirk adds: "If the 'strife' which symbolizes their interaction, and the consequent maintenance of the tension, ceased, then the world would cease to be—a consequence for which Heraclitus evidently rebukes Homer" (Fr. 27). Despite the self-refuting character of the alleged consequence, however, I think it can legitimately be questioned whether the consequence would logically follow in the sense that Kirk supposes. *If* the dominance of fire in an ἐκπύρωσις were to entail the destruction of all strife, then admittedly a situation would arise—an interval of absolute peace and rest—such as is expressly denied by several of Heraclitus' statements. But would a cosmic conflagration ever be absolute? Could it, in Heraclitus' terms of thinking, represent an interval of unalloyed oneness and unchallenged stasis? The very notion is repugnant to Heraclitus' style of thought. But could there not be a periodic cosmic conflagration without any implication of purity? There is nothing pure about the contrary cosmic situation—when a maximal amount of the fiery substance has transformed itself into water and earth. Why could there not be a counteractive situation, occurring at vastly long intervals, in which the universe somehow bursts into flame (as the doxographers have described the occurrence) with nothing more implied than that a maximal amount of the universal stuff (which is also process) has returned to a fiery condition? Surely the cosmic fiery state would have to be somehow impure in order to allow the seeds of a future universe to emerge from it. Even if the Upward Way is dominant during certain cosmic periods, still the tendencies of the Downward Way must always be somehow latent in it.

(2) and (3). The suggested reply to Kirk's first argument would have some relevance to the status of his second and third as well. The ambiguity of the phrase "by regular measures" is considered in the Note to Fr. 29 (Appendix B). Because of that ambiguity it is impossible to know whether the phrase argues for or against a belief in cosmic periods. Moreover, to say that cosmic process always has been and will be, is not to deny that there may be vast periods in which now one set of characteristics and now another predominates.

(4). What, then, of Plato's distinction, in *The Sophist*, between Heraclitus, who is said to have declared that unity and plurality exist simultaneously, and Empedocles, who is said to have held that these opposite states occur in temporal succession?[20] Presumably unity and plurality in this context refer, so far as Heraclitus is concerned, to fire on the one hand and the universe of individuated things on the other; and Kirk remarks that "no supporter of an ἐκπύρωσις in Heraclitus has been able to explain the testimony away." Nevertheless, one can observe that there are other places in the Dialogues where Plato is admittedly somewhat inaccurate and capricious in his historical references, and that there is some reason to suppose that his views on Heraclitus may have been taken from Heracliteans who were his contemporaries rather than from a textual study of the older philosopher's own writings.[21] In short, Plato's reference, although a stumbling block, is hardly a refutation.

Finally, Argument 5 is not a positive argument, but consists in saying that neither the evidence from Stoic opinions about Heraclitus nor the evidence from the canonical Fragments is conclusive.

On the other side of the controversy the most telling of the indirect evidences, in the form of testimonies that are not exact quotations, is found in Aristotle's *De Caelo*. Aristotle declares:

"That the world was generated all are agreed, but, the generation having occurred, some say that [the generated world] is eternal, others say that it is destructible like any other natural formation. Others again, with Empedocles of Acragas and Heraclitus of Ephesus, believe that there is alternation in the destructive process, which takes now this direction, now that, and continues without end."[22]

Since Aristotle here contrasts Heraclitus' position both with the belief that the world will last forever and with the belief that it will be destroyed once and for all, it must be that he takes Heraclitus to believe that the world will be destroyed and then will be created again, in a series of cosmic catastrophes and renewals, "continuing without end." The catastrophic phase of such a cycle, if Heraclitus believed in it, would be (whatever word he himself may have employed) what was later designated by the Stoic word ἐκπύρωσις. It is possible, of course, that Aristotle, as was suggested above in the case of Plato, might have erred in ascribing to Heraclitus opinions that were developed by certain self-styled Heracliteans of the fourth century. On the other hand there is no evidence, and I think no one has ever suggested, that the doctrine arose among Heracliteans of either Plato's or Aristotle's time. If the doctrine does not go back to Heraclitus himself, the usual alternative theory has been that it was of Stoic origin. Yet here is Aristotle, a generation before the advent of Stoicism, referring to the doctrine and evidently supposing that it dates back to Heraclitus a century and a half earlier. Does not Aristotle's apparent supposition, then, offer a reasonable, although by no means conclusive, ground for thinking that Heraclitus may have held, or at least may have speculated upon, the doctrine of periodic world conflagration?

There is another passage in Aristotle which indicates perhaps even more suggestively that he attributed the doctrine to Heraclitus. In the third book of the *Physics* he cites, perhaps even quotes (one cannot be sure), Heraclitus as saying that "at some time all things become fire." Now if this statement were taken by itself, it could be interpreted in either of two ways. It could be referring (1) to a general conflagration in which all things *together* enter into the fiery state, or (2) to the view that at different times different things come to the end of their individual existences and hence dissolve into the fire that is the basic constituent of everything. In short, it could be questioned whether "all things" is to be taken collectively or dissociatively. But the answer is made plain, it seems to me, by the context. Aristotle has just laid down the proposition that "neither fire nor any of the other elements can be infinite"—i.e., unlimited by the co-presence of other elements, other types of substance. That is to say, as he adds in the next sentence, "the All cannot either be or become any one of them." This is Aristotle's statement of his own view. He then adds, by way of contrast, Heraclitus' view that at some time all things *do* become fire.[23] There would be no point in introducing Heraclitus' opinion (or supposed opinion) here unless it were offered as opposed to the view upheld by Aristotle himself. Aristotle is declaring in the passage that the All, the entire universe, cannot possibly ever become a single substance such as fire, and he evidently means to cite Heraclitus as declaring on the contrary that at some time the All can and does become fire.

Although among the doxographers there are various later

references that attribute to Heraclitus a belief in periodic universal conflagration, such references have little independent value since it may well be that the information compiled by the doxographers stemmed, at least in large part, from information and opinions that were current in Aristotelian circles. The Aristotelian commentator Simplicius, in dealing with the above passage from *De Caelo*, epitomizes what he takes to be Heraclitus' doctrine in the words: "Periodically the universe bursts into flame and periodically it becomes extinguished." The fullest of such statements is made by Aëtius, as reconstructed by Diels from an epistle ascribed to Plutarch and from Stobaeus' *Eclogues*. The two versions, despite some minor differences, agree in attributing to Heraclitus and Hippasus jointly the view that "the universe and the bodies in it" are "dissolved by fire" in the general conflagration. Moreover, both versions introduce mention of the total fiery dissolution by the phrase, "then again"—evidently signifying that the general conflagration occurs not just once but repeatedly.[24] Other doxographical testimonies to much the same effect could be added. Such quotations show how widely in later ancient times it was customary among scholars to impute a belief in ἐκπύρωσις to Heraclitus. It is a possibility (nothing more) that those doxographers, or some of them, may have had the text of Heraclitus' treatise available to them; but it is also possible that they may have been simply repeating an unverified traditional interpretation.

In the face of these conflicting testimonies and evidences it is impossible to be certain today whether or not Heraclitus believed in a fiery periodicity of the universe. Among modern scholars Gomperz (the elder), Zeller, Gigon, Stock (the Aristotelian translator), and Mondolfo think that he did; Burnet, Fränkel, Cherniss, Kirk, and some others think that he did not. The question had better be regarded as an open one, and fortunately its solution is not required for an understanding of the essential points of Heraclitus' teaching, nor for an appreciation of their human significance.

The final Fragment of the present group (Fr. 41) serves as a transition to the material of the next chapter. It contains the only surviving statement of Heraclitus that is specifically about the nature of animal impulse. The anonymous Aristotelian author of *De Mundo* quite evidently understands the blow in question to mean a divine blow that goads the animal from within,[25] rather than the blow of a whip from outside. (It is quite possible, to be sure, that Heraclitus, who so often thinks plurisignatively, may have had the latter and more commonplace idea in mind as well, since it could serve as an outer visual symbol for the former.) Although the Aristotelian writer quotes the passage immediately after declaring that all animals are born, grow, and decay "in obedience to the ordinance of God," it is probable that as an Aristotelian he would not have had the idea of a personalized God in mind. If his phrase "obedience to the ordinance" is taken metaphorically, his view of God as the divine goad might be similar to the view of Heraclitus, except that Heraclitus pays more attention to the sudden, peculiar, and often self-warring ways in which the divine goad tends to manifest itself. Correspondingly, the good that is apprehended is relative (Frs. 99ff.), and when it acts—whether for the weal or woe of the agent—it is likely to resemble the blow of a whip in its sharpness and unexpectedness. Such animal impulse, on the threshold of awareness, is intermediate between the fiery activity that is ever going on in the physical world and the fire of self-enlightenment, to which the conscious mind can rise by self-examination (Fr. 8) and by listening to the Logos (Fr. 2), which is at once other than and yet one with the individual self.

CHAPTER IV

HUMAN SOUL

mysterious depths

42. *You could not discover the limits of soul, even if you traveled every road to do so; such is the depth of its meaning.*

(43. *[Soul] is the vaporization out of which everything else is derived; moreover it is the least corporeal of things and is in ceaseless flux, for the moving world can only be known by what is in motion.*)

44. *Souls are vaporized from what is moist.*

45. *Soul has its own principle of growth.*

46. *A dry soul is wisest and best.*

47. *Souls take pleasure in becoming moist.*

48. *A drunken man has to be led by a young boy, whom he follows stumbling and not knowing whither he goes, for his soul is moist.*

49. *It is death to souls to become water, and it is death to water to become earth. Conversely, water comes into existence out of earth, and souls out of water.*

50. *Even the sacred barley drink separates when it is not stirred.*

51. *It is hard to fight against impulsive desire; whatever it wants it will buy at the cost of soul.*

52. *It would not be better if things happened to men just as they wish.*

53. *Although it is better to hide our ignorance, this is hard to do when we relax over wine.*

54. *A foolish man is a-flutter at every word.*

55. *Fools, although they hear, are like the deaf; to them the adage applies that when present they are absent.*

56. *Bigotry is the sacred disease.*

57. *Most people do not take heed of the things they encounter, nor do they grasp them even when they have learned about them, although they suppose they do.*

*58. If all existing things were smoke, it is by smell that we
would distinguish them.*

59. In Hades souls perceive by smelling.

60. Corpses are more fit to be thrown out than dung.

THE question of soul is primarily the question of what it is to
be alive—not as life is observed externally in other organisms,
but as it is known by one who lives and is reflectively aware
of himself as living. But while self-awareness is the most
essential step in coming to know what life means, it must be
accompanied by another. Men are not solipsists, and no one,
however much of an egoist he may be, ever knows merely
himself alone. Souls form communities, and one's growing
awareness of what it is to be oneself is somehow bound up
with a growing recognition of the other centers of awareness
by which one is surrounded. Accordingly our knowledge of
soul is at once inward and outward. The inward discovery is
of first importance to one who seeks a sound philosophical
method (Fr. 8), but the present group of Fragments implies
an interplay of both procedures.

A first task, in seeking to understand Heraclitus' view of
soul, is to decide upon the most nearly adequate translation
for the Greek word ψυχή. Three English words suggest themselves : soul, psyche, and self. "Soul" has been the traditional
translation, but the objection to it is that in many persons'
minds the word has become entangled with certain theological
and eschatological concepts, particularly those of divine creation and immortality. It is even possible to hear sometimes
the opinion expressed that the soul does not or may not exist
—an opinion which can usually be found to represent the
speaker's loose and inaccurate way of rejecting the supposed
theological implications of the word. Now to deny or doubt
the existence of the soul is to have lost precise contact with
the meaning of ψυχή as the word is employed by the more
reflective Greek writers who are not hampered by a dogma,
notably Heraclitus and Aristotle. There is a sense, if one

narrows it down carefully, in which it is impossible to doubt that the thinker or doubter does in fact exist at the moment of doubting, and it has been a primary task of philosophical analysis to indicate exactly what that sense is. If "soul" could be taken to mean only the sense of being and being aware in a certain milieu of observable events, without any implicit postulation regarding origin, status, or destiny, the word would be a satisfactory one; but it has become suspect in many quarters today because of the associations that cling to it. Some modern writers, therefore, prefer to substitute the anglicized word "psyche"—thinking, no doubt, that this, with its down-to-earth ring, is free from adventitious connotations. They probably delude themselves, however; for if "soul" carries an overtone of church and Sunday School, "psyche" suggests no less forcibly the psychology laboratory and the mental health clinic. Such associations are unintentional, but they are likely to saddle the thinker who uses them with implications that he has not fully examined. The word "self" is probably freer from such difficulties than either of the other two, although to the minds of some it might carry an individualistic emphasis, suggesting perhaps subconsciously the word "selfish" as its apparent cognate. Of course, when this word is chosen such connotations must be avoided, for our language should not be allowed to rule out the possibility that souls may merge, partly or wholly, either with other souls or with a more universal and divine soulhood. The important thing is to choose and contextualize our words in such a way as not to prejudge any of the questions that may arise, and this requires constant vigilance. All in all, it seems to me wisest to translate the Greek word ψυχή by the word "soul" in the Fragments, occasionally varying it with "self" in the exposition that follows.

Another point to be noted about Heraclitus' use of the word is that except in Fr. 48 he never employs the article with it. When the word occurs in the plural (Frs. 44, 47, 49) there is no problem of translation, for our English idiom allows us

to speak of "souls" without the article. Also in Fr. 46 there
is no problem, for here the use of the indefinite article (which
is nonexistent in Greek) seems to be the most idiomatic way
of fitting up the sentence in English. In Fr. 48, which is the
only instance where the definite article is employed, the context justifies the translation, "his soul." But in Frs. 42, 43,
45, and 51 the absence of the article in English may sound a
bit queer. Translators have sometimes yielded to the temptation of smoothing out the English by writing "the soul" in
these instances (as Fairbanks does with Fr. 42, Lattimore
with Frs. 42 and 51, and Freeman with Frs. 42, 45, and 51),
but such a compromise brings into the English an air of
definiteness and a connotation of substantiality which are not
present in the Greek. Here it is necessary to recall the discussion in the Introduction, about certain ambiguities that are
inherent in the language and basic conceptions of Heraclitus'
time—in particular, the ambiguity between the noun and
other parts of speech. "Soul," for Heraclitus, is almost a
noun; it is more of a noun than it is anything else. Yet by
employing it without the article he avoids a full grammatical
commitment, and the noun in the four instances mentioned
hovers on the brink of being an adjective, perhaps also a
verb. The phrase, "the soul," is likely to carry, for a modern
reader, brought up (however loosely) on Christian notions,
a suggestion of permanence—which, of course, is absent from
Heraclitus' conception. Soul, to Heraclitus, is quality, substance, and activity in one. It is undoubtedly something real,
and indeed of utmost importance (for it is only by being a
soul, in the broad sense, that one can raise questions about
souls or anything else); nevertheless we should avoid being
trapped by accidents of grammar and idiom into saying too
much about it.

Since Heraclitus is building a cosmology, it becomes necessary for him to consider how soul is related to other elements
in the fluctuating universe. In Fr. 44 souls are said to have
their origin in what is moist, being vaporized from the

moisture; and in Fr. 43, on the authority of Aristotle, soul is said to *be* a process of vaporization. The word ἀναθυμίασις in Fr. 43 and its cognate form in Fr. 44 both connote a vaporization that is warm, or hot, or even fiery. For as remarked earlier, the transformation from water into air and the transformation from air into fire tended to be regarded as continuous phases of a single process, exemplifying the Upward Way. Heraclitus and his contemporaries were not accustomed to distinguish clearly between vaporization and bursting into flame; the latter phenomenon they evidently saw as the completion and natural outcome of the former. In naïvely visual terms vapor looks like smoke, and smoke suggests fire; this points to the upward way. On the other hand, so far as vapor is moist it therein reveals its countertendency to move along the downward way, transforming itself into water and, if the tendency persists, into mud and earth. Soul, then, has its natural place somewhere in the area between water and fire, and contains within itself the possibilities of self-transformation in either direction. That peculiar in-between state, allowing it to change itself or undergo change in either of two directions, is identified by Heraclitus with those stages in nature's up-and-down process which show themselves as vapor, smoke, and fiery exhalation.

With the soul and its self-transforming power thus conceived in naturalistic perspective, it is easier to see what is meant by Fr. 46 on the one hand and by Frs. 47, 48, and 49 on the other. Since soul is a dynamical something, always tending by a sort of inner urgency to become other than what it was and is, it may (if it be wise and excellent) struggle upwards to become drier, brighter, and more fiery, or (if it yields to degeneration) it may slip downwards to become more sodden and moist. In Aristotelian language the soul is a potency that can actualize itself, more or less, in either of the two directions. Heraclitus' vocabulary was not capable of expressing so logically abstract a distinction as that of Aristotle between potentiality and actuality; but one of the most impressive marks of his genius lies in his ability to reach out for, and darkly adumbrate, ideas that are beyond the natural semantic range of his somewhat primitive language.

The situation is somewhat complicated by the fact that in the main doxographical passage from which Fr. 44 is taken, the Fragment appears as a codicil to the famous remark about the impossibility of stepping twice into the same river (Fr. 21). As reported by Arius Didymus the total passage runs as follows: "To those who step into the same rivers, other waters are continually flowing on. And souls are vaporized from what is moist." It is hard to see any clear connection between the two sentences; and therefore I have judged it best to present them separately as distinct Fragments in the present arrangement. Nevertheless, the words with which Arius Didymus introduces the double passage suggest that he saw a connection or was trying to see one. What he says is: "Wishing to make clear that the souls, as they rise up in vapor, become intellectually aware, he [Heraclitus] represents them in the likeness of rivers, speaking thus , . ."; and then comes the double quotation. Although this explanation may seem to confuse the matter more than ever, I think that perhaps a further clue may be found in another passage from Arius, in which he attributes to Heraclitus the view that soul is "a perceptive exhalation."[1] Evidently, by one metaphor and another, Heraclitus is trying to convey the idea that the soul comes into existence out of certain moist elements in nature (possibly he may have in mind the moisture of the maternal womb), and that the mystery of emergent selfhood, which no theory can ever satisfactorily explain, can be described figuratively as a being exhaled or vaporized from that generative moisture. Aristotle, in *De Anima*, employs a more developed philosophical vocabulary to grapple with the same problem; but I cannot see that his characterization of the affections of the soul as "meanings ($\lambda \acute{o} \gamma o \iota$) subsisting in matter"[2] comes any closer to the heart of the problem than Heraclitus' more naïvely picturesque representation had managed to do.

But while the naturalistic perspective furnishes an essential part of the truth about soul, it does not and cannot furnish the entire truth. Two contrasting and mutually irreducible aspects of soul must be considered together, if Heraclitus' doctrine is to be understood. On the one hand, soul is an emergent and finite phenomenon of the natural world; it is born out of moisture, and eventually (although not necessarily at the moment of what we call death) it will pass away again. On the other hand a soul, during the span of time in which it is alive, possesses a real though limited autonomy. In this connection Fr. 45 is significant; for to say that a soul has its own principle of growth is to say that it must be understood not as being pushed into activity from without, but as bestirring itself from within—like a fire rekindling itself from a tiny spark. One can know what soul is only by having gone through such a process of self-rekindling. Soul, which is to say selfhood, is unique in that it alone has the double property of existing and of knowing its own existence. In the history of philosophical speculations materialism has taken the one aspect as basic, idealism the other. But in Heraclitus' view neither of these opposing systems of thought is comprehensive enough to express the truth. For reality, he holds, is paradoxical at bottom (Fr. 17); and that out of which everything else is formed (Fr. 43) can surely not be known by any single kind of intellectual maneuver (Fr. 42). That soul is a more or less accidental product of the natural world and that soul is somehow significantly self-determining are two warring but ineradicable truths about soul, which an awakened intellect will always hold in unresolved tension.

The principle that the soul must strive toward the fullest possible activity in order to know truly, is differently represented by the contrasting metaphors of dryness and moisture (Frs. 46, 47) and by the analogy of the sacred mixed drink (Fr. 50). The peculiar concoction which the word κυκεών denotes was a ceremonial beverage made of barley, grated cheese, and Pramnian wine, and obviously these ingredients tend to separate when the drink is allowed to stand. The very character of the beverage can be maintained only by constant stirring. Theophrastus, who quotes the passage, introduces it with the explanation that there are certain things which hold together only by being in motion, and which lose their essential nature when the motion ceases.[3] Of course the general Heraclitean position is that all things without exception have their being in motion; nevertheless the principle is more conspicuously true of some things than of others, and it is especially and most significantly true of human selves. To hold on stubbornly to one's way of life is to lose it; whereas to live always on the verge, always in readiness for whatever may come, "expecting the unexpected," is to meet life on its own terms and thus to become one with it in the only way that is possible, through yielding oneself up to its law of continual change. An unstirred self, like an unstirred barley-drink, tends to decompose, breaking up into dregs of material impulse on the one hand and ghostly ideal aspirations on the other. The perceptions and ideas arising from such a state of affairs tend to become illusory. Truth about the variegated and paradoxical world we live in can come to us only as our thoughts and sensitivities are constantly entering into new amalgams.

The ethical tone of Frs. 46 to 51 stands in sharp contrast to the statement (Fr. 108) that the way up and the way down are one and the same. The present Fragments affirm that the upward way toward light, dryness, and intellectual awareness is preferable to the downward way toward moisture and drunken muddle. What, in view of this avowal, is meant by the seeming indifferentism of the later Fragment? The solution must be found in the different perspectives that the two kinds of statement represent—the one ethical and personal, the other cosmological and universal. In the perspective of here and now, with a choice of paths before me, it is pertinent to judge one path better than the other; in fact, a failure to do so is even self-delusory, because a self that tries to avoid choosing makes a choice in that very avoidance, in letting its action be determined by dark impulses instead of by lighted reason. A self in its awareness knows the difference between climbing and slipping, and it knows that the former alternative represents its fulfillment, and that the latter represents intrinsic defeat. On the other hand, each moral struggle and moral choice, and the unique truth it expresses, is embedded in time as an event amidst innumerable other events. From the cosmic point of view the individual event, whatever its quality and temporal importance, is insignificant; the implicit attitude is symbolized by the divine child recklessly moving counters in a game (Fr. 24). Of all the paradoxes in Heraclitus' philosophy there is none more fundamental than this one of the simultaneous validity of the two attitudes, valuational and trans-valuational.

The statements about smelling (Frs. 58, 59) require some remark. The obvious implication is that souls in Hades are composed of smoke, and that for this reason they must perceive and be perceived by smelling and being smelled.[4] The curious hypothesis is another consequence of Heraclitus' view, mentioned earlier, that smoke, cloud, and vapor are but different forms of the state of things intermediate between fire and water, and that soul belongs ontologically in this area. Being vaporous a soul is also smoky, and the question underlying the two Fragments is, What kind of awareness is possible in a disembodied, hence a smoky state? The answer given is that as ghosts we could no longer perceive and discriminate by sight, touch, and hearing, but only by smell. Heraclitus appears to be reaching toward the idea that there are modes of existence essentially different from that of the familiar world which we come to know by familiar means. Perhaps this interpretation suggests a new and not altogether reassuring twist to what is suggested by Fr. 67. Truly the question of what it is to be a self is a very deep mystery (Fr. 42); and Heraclitus is suggesting that there may be aspects of the mystery, totally ungraspable in our present state of being, which may become temporarily known to us, temporarily even a part of us, in some mode of being that succeeds the shock of death. The main evidences of Heraclitus' view upon this subject are to be found in the next group of Fragments.

CHAPTER V

IN RELIGIOUS PERSPECTIVE

61. *Human nature has no real understanding; only the divine nature has it.*

(62. *Man is not rational; only what encompasses him is intelligent.*)

63. *What is divine escapes men's notice because of their incredulity.*

64. *Although intimately connected with the Logos, men keep setting themselves against it.*

65. *As in the nighttime a man kindles for himself (ἅπτεται) a light, so when a living man lies down in death with his vision extinguished he attaches himself (ἅπτεται) to the state of death; even as one who has been awake lies down with his vision extinguished and attaches himself to the state of sleep.*

66. *Immortals become mortals, mortals become immortals; they live in each other's death and die in each other's life.*

67. *There await men after death such things as they neither expect nor have any conception of.*

68. *They arise into wakefulness and become guardians of the living and the dead.*

69. *A man's character is his guardian divinity.*

70. *Greater dooms win greater destinies.*

71. *Justice will overtake fabricators of lies and false witnesses.*

72. *Fire in its advance will judge and overtake all things.*

73. *How can anyone hide from that which never sets?*

(74. When some visitors unexpectedly found Heraclitus warming himself by the cooking fire: *Here, too, are gods.*)

75. *They pray to images, much as if they should talk to houses; for they do not know the nature of gods and heroes.*

76. *Night-walkers, magicians, bacchantes, revellers, and participants in the mysteries! What are regarded as mysteries among men are unholy rituals.*

77. *Their processions and their phallic hymns would be disgraceful exhibitions, were it not that they are done in honor of Dionysus. But Dionysus, in whose honor they rave and hold big feasts, is the same as Hades.*

78. *When defiled they purify themselves with blood—as though one who had stepped into filth should wash himself with filth. If any of his fellowmen should perceive him acting in such a way, they would regard him as mad.*

79. *The Sibyl with raving mouth utters solemn, unadorned, unlovely words, but she reaches out over a thousand years with her voice because of the god in her.*

HUMAN SOULS or selves exist not only in relation to the material substratum from which they have been vaporized; they exist also in significant relation, or in possibility of significant relation, to the divine Logos that permeates all things—which is to say, all activities. There is a passage in Sextus Empiricus which, although it does not appear to be meant as an exact quotation, is offered as a statement of Heraclitus' doctrine on this point. Sextus begins by quoting Euripides' address to Zeus in *The Trojan Women*: "To see into thy nature, O Zeus, is baffling to the mind. I have been praying to thee without knowing whether thou art necessity or nature or simply the intelligence of mortals."[1] The divine reality which may be called by the name of Zeus (when the name is employed seriously and not with mythological flippancy) is not other than what Heraclitus symbolizes as the divine Logos; and the passage from Euripides is joined in Sextus' text with the following paraphrase of a part of Heraclitus' doctrine:

"So it is by in-breathing the divine Logos that we become intelligent, according to Heraclitus. During sleep we are forgetful, but we become mindful again on waking up. For in sleep the pores of the senses are closed, so that the mind in us is shut off from what is akin to it in the surrounding world, and its connection with outer things is preserved only at a vegetative level through the pores of the skin. Being thus cut off it loses its formative power of memory. But when we wake up again, it peers out through the pores of the senses, which serve as little windows, and by thus entering into relation with what surrounds us it regains the power of reason."[2]

While there is a possibility that Sextus may be supplementing Heraclitus' doctrine of the superiority of waking consciousness over sleep by adding a physiological explanation of his own, at any rate the explanation seems to be consistent enough with Heraclitus' known teachings, and thus it may be taken as either a paraphrase or a natural development of what he said. Whatever the exact physiological process may be, the important thing for Heraclitus is that in sleep, as well as in mystical trances, we become deceived by dreams and hallucinations (Frs. 15, 16); only in waking periods, and in the most intensely alive of them, can we achieve some momentary glimpse of what truly *is*.

There is a further remark which Sextus makes shortly after the passage just quoted; and I add it because, once again, it seems to be intended as a characterization of Heraclitus' view, and in any case is not out of line with it. Sextus writes:

"Just as coals when brought close to the fire undergo a change that renders them incandescent, while if moved away they become extinguished; so likewise that portion of the surrounding milieu that is making a sojourn in the body, in losing contact with the surrounding milieu, therein loses its rational character by the separation, for its only communion with the outer universe now takes place through the body's very numerous pores."

The idea is that the self becomes most intensely alive and aware not in isolation, which can only breed illusions, but when it is most keenly alert to what is going on in the world around it—alert in such a way that like smouldering coals it draws into itself more fiery substance from the enveloping fire.

The last of this preliminary series of statements by which Sextus characterizes the doctrine of Heraclitus has already been mentioned in Chapter I, but it deserves to be reconsidered in the present context. Sextus writes:

> "So Heraclitus asserts that the common and divine Logos, by participation in which we become rational, is the criterion of truth."

The latter part of Fr. 43, supplemented by Frs. 46 and 50, has now thrown further light upon the meaning of the statement. Participation in the Logos is not self-isolation and it is not stultification of the intelligence; on the contrary, since the Logos is the principle of continual motion and change, which is also symbolized by the divine fire, it can only be by making our souls dry and fiery, our perceptions keen, and our wills unsubjected to cloying emotions, that we can really participate in the Logos instead of feeding our fancies with mythological vulgarizations of it. Such real participation, through mental alertness to the ever-changing but objective world, is what provides us with the criterion of truth.

In speaking of Heraclitus' religious philosophy, or of the religious dimension of his philosophy, we must avoid the familiar Christian associations that are likely, even in disguised form, to cling to the word. There is no supposition in Heraclitus' thought of a single universal God who is at once personal, omniscient, and (despite all appearances to the contrary) deeply concerned about the ultimate destiny of mankind in general and, for better or worse, of each particular human individual. There is, to be sure, in Heraclitus' view, a unity and coherence that is somehow present as a hidden other aspect of the plurality and diversity of things that is seen everywhere, and he even goes so far as to describe that cosmic oneness as "wisdom" (Fr. 119) and "intelligence" (Fr. 120). Such words, however, express a metaphor intended to suggest the mysterious organizing power that pervades the universe as a whole, manifesting unlimited possibilities of comeback after defeat and of new creation after destruction and death. If we interpret the metaphor literally, we ·shall overstress the human analogy implied in the ideas of wisdom and intelligence, and thus shall fall into anthropomorphism. Xenophanes, as remarked in the Introduction, had struck a new note in Greek religious philosophy by ridiculing the human and even racial characteristics that have variously been ascribed to God, by speculating that if oxen could paint they would represent God in the likeness of oxen,[3] and by insisting that God in his true nature must transcend all such characteristics. No doubt Heraclitus had been influenced by Xenophanes' teaching in his youth; at any rate in his mature philosophy he carries the principle still further. Granted, the surviving fragments of Xenophanes are so sparse that the full extent of his innovations is uncertain; but there is no evidence that he pursued the ethical implications of his doctrine. God, he declares, is not to be pictured as snub-nosed in the manner of the Ethiopians, or as blue-eyed and red-haired in the manner of the Thracians, or as moving about from place to place; there is nothing said, however, about God being beyond good and evil. It was left for Heraclitus to take this final step, to which the rigorous logic of transcendence would have to lead. For whenever we ascribe ethical characteristics to God we inevitably appeal to idols of the tribe, and usually of the marketplace too. God is, we tend to think, on the side of men as against tigers, snakes, and deadly germs (evidence to the contrary notwithstanding), and even, at a proper time in history, on the side of democracies as against dictatorships. Such partisan views, in one form or another, tend to recommend themselves to the popular imagination whenever ·it concerns itself briefly with religious matters. The grounds for them, however, become increasingly flimsy when one examines them philosophically without the rosy lenses that our fears and hopes usually contrive to set before our vision. To speak seriously of God's transcendence is to suggest that he has a nature that is independent of our images and conceptions of him, and to ask unflinchingly what that nature is. The way of philosophy is to do just that, and Heraclitus was above all else a philosopher. If God is truly God and universal, then he must be the God of all that exists and moves and struggles in any way whatever—the God alike of gnats and vipers, of angels and devils, men and mice, Christians and cannibals, creative genius and destructive cataclysm, without showing any special and prolonged favoritism to any of them. A sort of intelligence displays itself in God's nature and operations, Heraclitus observes, but it is an intelligence only remotely and abstractly like anything we know on the human level, and we shall mistake it profoundly if we allow any further human associations to color our description of it. Now in judging that the divine intelligence is so utterly different from our everyday intelligence, we are likening it, from the human partisan standpoint, to something vastly indifferent and irresponsible, like a child arbitrarily moving counters in a game (Fr. 24). This, too, is a metaphor of course, but it is usefully corrective of certain other and more familiar metaphors that tend to influence our thinking. In particular it is a metaphor that should be remembered when reading the Fragments in which Heraclitus ascribes oneness, intelligence, and godhead to the cosmic All. Statements about the universe are but half-truths—true and false at the same time, as Heraclitus likes to say—and the statement that intelligence guides the universe must be balanced by the counter-statements that the thunderbolt pilots all things (Fr. 35) and that "the royal power is a child's" (Fr. 24).

When the word "gods" is used in the plural Heraclitus is speaking about something quite different from the ultimate cosmic mystery. Fr. 74, the only one requiring stage directions, evokes a charming picture of Heraclitus, despite his later reputation as a gloomy and forbidding philosopher, meeting the situation with light grace when, on a certain occasion, some visitors found him warming himself by the kitchen stove. It was not a place where a Greek gentleman would normally have been found, and to a lesser man some explanation might have seemed to be called for. Heraclitus, who was not one to be bound by petty rules of etiquette, remarked simply, "Here, too, are gods." The notion that gods are everywhere, or at any rate are to be found in unexpected places, was not new with Heraclitus. Nearly a century before him Thales had declared that all things are full of gods. Aristotle, in quoting the remark, takes it to mean that "soul is diffused throughout the entire universe"; Simplicius, commenting on the passage in Aristotle, takes Thales' statement to mean that "the gods are blended with all things," and he adds his own opinion that "this is strange."[4] The idea is strange enough at first sight, no doubt, but it becomes less so when it is examined without mythological preconceptions of what the nature of gods must be. To be blended with gods evidently meant in the sixth century much the same thing as to be blended with soul; for Aristotle reports that Thales reasoned that the magnet must be imbued with soul because it causes motion in the iron. Evidently, then, Thales believed that while the gods, or centers of soul-force, are everywhere, they are more active or more conspicuous in some things than in others. There is nothing in the view that is inconsistent with Heraclitus' known utterances, and quite possibly he held something very like it, but unfortunately there is a shortage of available Fragments that bear clearly upon the point.

Two beliefs of Heraclitus are fairly evident, however: first, that gods are higher types of being than men are (Fr. 104); secondly, that gods are nevertheless finite and mortal. The latter belief is clear from Fr. 66: "Immortals become mortals, mortals become immortals; they live in each other's death and die in each other's life." The words "immortals" and "mortals" are traditional synonyms for gods and men respectively; Heraclitus' preference for the more paradoxical form of expression is characteristic of him. Of course in strict logic it is impossible that anything immortal should ever become mortal, for if it were to do so it could not have been truly immortal in the first place; and vice versa. But in the universe as Heraclitus envisages it there is nothing truly immortal in the literal sense—except, indeed, the endless process of mortality itself. The meaning of the passage appears to be, then, that in the whirligig of universal change there comes a time when a god dies and the soul-force that constituted him turns into something else, quite possibly into a man; likewise men, when they die, may turn into gods or something like gods for a while. This interpretation of the passage is confirmed by Clement of Alexandria; for the version that he gives of the passage is simply, "Men become gods, gods become men." (The verb, in both versions, is omitted and is left for the reader to supply.) It seems likely that Hippolytus' version, which is employed in Fr. 66, is the more authentic one—for reasons discussed at the beginning of Appendix B. At any rate, whatever the original verbal expression may have been, it seems evident enough that Heraclitus believed that there occur, at least in some instances, metamorphoses of men into gods and of gods into men.

Now if men become gods it must be that they do so after the end of human life, and that therefore the soul or self must survive death in some way or other. Although certain scholars have denied that Heraclitus believed in the survival of the soul after death, on the ground that the soul like everything else must be in constant flux, I do not see how his acceptance of such a belief can be denied when the evidence of Frs. 59, 65, 66, 67, 68, and possibly 70 is fully considered. The question here is of survival, not of immortality. The older distinction between the two ideas has become lost in modern Christendom, where the notion of a future life, whether affirmed or denied, ordinarily carries with it the idea of immortality, which is to say of ultimate deathlessness and eternal life. Naturally it would be inconsistent with Heraclitus' philosophical position to say that any soul lasts forever.

Nothing lasts forever, except activity. Nevertheless, even in a ceaselessly fluctuating universe some things last longer than others. In Plato's *Phaedo*, after it has been agreed that the soul probably survives the death of the body, the question comes up as to whether the soul might not possibly outlive several bodies in which it was reincarnated and yet finally perish, much as a man might successively wear out several garments and yet die in the end.[5] Despite Socrates' specious refutation of the proposal it was a more plausible hypothesis to Greek thinkers than it usually is to us, and the evidence seems to be that Heraclitus believed in something of that sort.

But if Heraclitus held a theory of survival, as I believe he did, his indications of the nature of that survival are tantalizingly incomplete in the Fragments. There is his general remark that the experiences awaiting a person after death are so utterly strange as to defy previous conception or expectation (Fr. 67), which gives a more specific application to the general truth uttered in Fr. 19. If our awareness continues beyond death at all, it may find the ghostly state a very unexpected one indeed, and many an ancient philosopher has warned against encumbering ourselves at the threshold of death by clinging to any preconceived notions of what is to come. Fr. 68, "They arise into wakefulness and become guardians of the living and the dead," is difficult to interpret because of the impossibility of discovering just what "they" refers to. Evidently not to the dead in general, because these unidentified ones are to have dominion over the living and the dead alike. Perhaps they are the souls who in life have refrained from becoming moist and have made themselves into dry lights.

Fragment 65 offers one of the most mysterious statements, and I suspect one of the most important, in all the extant Heraclitean corpus. Numerous variant readings and interpretations have been proposed, a few of which are mentioned in Appendix B. Fairbanks' well-known translation, based upon Bywater's overcautiously edited version of the text, "Man, like a light in the night, is kindled and put out," expresses a rather banal idea and loses the gist of what Heraclitus is saying. The present translation is based upon a restored version of the traditional text, as explained in Appendix B; and it indicates, I believe, darkly but in a way that no other Fragment does, one indispensable aspect of Heraclitus' deeply paradoxical view of the nature of death.

The most obvious fact about the Fragment is that it hinges upon a serious pun. The verb ἅπτειν in the active voice means both "fasten" or "attach" and also "kindle" or "set fire to." Any Greek lexicon gives both meanings as a matter of course. In the middle voice, which is employed on at least the first two of the word's three appearances in the present Fragment, the first of these meanings would become "attach oneself to"; the second would become either "strike a light for oneself" or "kindle oneself," "burst into flame." Now the opening clause of the Fragment is clear enough: as the basis of comparison it describes the action of a man at nightfall kindling a light for himself because his vision is impaired by the darkness. It is the next occurrence of the verb that is crucial. On the surface it makes a pun, and thus the middle part of the Fragment may be taken to say: "Similarly a living man, when his vision is extinguished by death, *attaches himself to* the state of death" (literally, to [the state of] a dead man). But if this were the entire meaning, the statement would be trivial and the pun would be a childish trick. So simple an interpretation is unacceptable; for Heraclitus, even at his wittiest, is always deeply in earnest. The solution, I believe, is that the verb on its second occurrence carries two meanings at once: in addition to the meaning just given there is connoted the further idea of lighting oneself up, of bursting into flame. This second meaning, when applied to the sentence, produces the following translation: "Similarly a living man, when his [human] vision is extinguished in death, *flares into flame* on achieving the state of death." The first meaning is the principal one; the second is a semantic overtone, intended lightly and yet seriously—at once a question mark and a reminder that there is always another and opposite side to every situation, and that there is always more than meets the eye in anything so essential and ontologically primary as the transition known as death. The mystery of death is not something that can be expressed in straightforward language. All such language carries with it associations that have been developed out of the familiar experiences of everyday human life; how, then, could it possibly be adequate to describe the nature of something so utterly unfamiliar and mysteriously transhuman as after-death experience, which "we can neither expect nor have any conception of" (Fr. 67)? Heraclitus, like every serious poet, perceives the limited expressiveness of everyday language and employs certain devices, particularly metaphor and paradox, for pointing, however uncertainly, beyond it. His use of the verb on its second occurrence in the Fragment, then, is plurisignative;[6] the reader's mind is challenged to think in two directions at once—a challenge that must sometimes be present in all good writing.

The final clause of the Fragment is less important, and looks like an afterthought, thrown in for good measure. It does not seem to me to clarify the strange, complex, and intentionally ambiguous point of the central clause; but there it is, and we must make of it what we can. The principal question about it is, how to interpret the verb, which occurs for the third time here. Does it carry on the double meaning from the previous instance? Although a sure reply is impossible, I would think not. Heraclitus has declared forcibly that any seeming illumination in the state of sleep is merely private dream, not real awareness (Frs. 15, 16). Granted that he might characteristically have in mind some contrary aspect of the matter, and that sleep despite its sogginess might yet emit sparkles of flame, nevertheless there is no warrant in the existent Fragments for asserting such an interpretation. On the basis of the fragmentary evidence of Heraclitus' teachings we had better assume that the verb on its third occasion means simply "attach oneself" or "become attached" and does not mean "burst into flame." An incidental result of this interpretation would be to discover a neat little structure in the semantic variations of the verb: at first it would mean only lighting, then both attaching and lighting, then only attaching. It is also possible that Heraclitus intends the final meaning to be in the passive rather than the middle voice; for in the present tense, which is employed, the two voices would be grammatically indistinguishable. The final clause would then read: "even as one who has been awake becomes joined with the state of sleep." But it seems likely that Heraclitus, having preceded the age of grammarians, would not explicitly have thought of the distinction between middle and passive where there was no difference in grammatical form, and that consequently the meaning in the present instance would straddle the distinction.

But the foregoing interpretation of Fr. 65 leaves us with a conundrum: how to reconcile the notion of death that it appears to imply with the notion implicit in Fr. 49? The one Fragment envisages death as a flaring up in flame, the other identifies it with passage into a watery state. The one sees death in the perspective of the upward, the other in the perspective of the downward way. Does Heraclitus mean that some souls at death go one way, some the other? This is evidently Kirk's answer, for he writes:

"If, then, when the body dies the soul either becomes water or remains fiery, and becomes more fiery still, what is the factor which determines this issue? Clearly, the composition of the soul at the moment of death; ... if the amount of water at the moment of death exceeds the amount of fire, presumably the soul as a whole suffers the 'death' of turning into water: but if the soul is predominantly 'dry,' then it escapes the 'death' of becoming water and joins the world-mass of fire. This is deduction, but I think permissible deduction."[7]

With this interpretation of Kirk's I would agree on the whole, but with the speculative qualification that perhaps a soul might undergo both processes at once. The upward and downward ways are simultaneously active in every soul, although to different degrees, and every soul is in some state of tension between upward and downward pulls. All things being in a state of change, souls included, it may be that the warring elements in a soul pull apart sharply at death, the one part flaring up like a light in the nighttime, the other part sinking coldly into a watery and earthy inertness.

Perhaps the foregoing interpretation may throw some light upon the meaning of Frs. 71, 72, and 73. Since the first and third of them are quoted by Clement of Alexandria and the second by Hippolytus, there have been critics who have discounted the quotations on the ground that these Christian writers might have touched them up for their own evangelical purposes. But Clement and Hippolytus, whatever their general intent, were not using Heraclitus evangelistically: they quoted him as a pagan philosopher, and Hippolytus did so with the further aim of showing him to be at the root of a heresy that had crept into Christianity. There does not seem to have been much reason why they should have misquoted him, and moreover there is cumulative evidence that Hippolytus, for one, quotes (however he may afterwards interpret) with accuracy and care. Now the quotation given by Hippolytus is, "Fire in its advance will judge and condemn all things"; and if this can be accepted as a genuine utterance of Heraclitus there should be no difficulty about accepting the two quotations by Clement, for all three of them are in much the same vein.

But of course, in order to accept the three quotations as authoritative it is necessary to be able to see how they fit, even though not tightly, into Heraclitus' otherwise known cosmology. Now the fundamental principle to keep in mind when reading any of his utterances is that everything has another and contrary aspect, to be seen only by a mind that is active enough to be able to step into a sometimes wildly different perspective from the one with which it started. There is no such thing as the *merely* physical; that is a conceptual abstraction that men have developed as one of the instruments of a technological age. The Heraclitean fire, as we have seen, is at once physical and more than physical: it has a psychical aspect (as inner quickening and illumination), a metaphysical aspect (as eternal process), and a moral aspect. Now if Heraclitus believed in cosmic cycles—a possibility discussed in Chapter III—then at those periods of time when the cosmic fire flares up into utter conflagration, there is still a plural significance involved. Fire, at such crises in the life of the cosmos, consumes all things, but it may do so in either of two ways. It may burn the individual to a cinder or it may assimilate him to its own being. Perhaps, in some way that eludes our schematic understanding, it will operate upon us in both respects at once; for every person's soul is divided, and to some degree everyone is groping toward the light and sinking into earthiness at the same time. Salvation and damnation are not clearly distinguished states, the one allotted to certain fortunate individuals and the other to certain unfortunate ones. The two destinies represent the eternally warring factions of the human soul, with its simultaneous yearning for the light and propensity for mud. To carry out Heraclitus' metaphor we must think of mud as inflammable, but our thermonuclear discoveries have removed any difficulty on that score. In any case, the tenor of the metaphor of light and mud is ourselves, and the central question is, which of them we shall most essentially be. Our choice, which in some sense is made anew at each waking moment, develops a special corollary in the day of the great conflagration. For the issue then is, to each conscious being, whether he is to be flame or cinder. A literal restatement of the metaphor would be misleading; each one who would find the meaning must do so by looking to his own depths and resources.

At all events, when the ultimate cosmic situation is considered in terms of the perennial choice that lies before each conscious individual, the appropriateness of Frs. 71, 72, and 73 to the Heraclitean philosophy becomes more evident. We do not know the original context of Fr. 71, but we may assume that liars and false witnesses were mentioned merely as instances, and not the most important instances, of men choosing the downward way. The essence of the downward way, in what may be called (descriptively, not melodramatically) the catastrophic perspective, is to become a victim of the Event through attachment to the temporal things and attitudes that it will destroy. The fire as it advances is at once physical fact and divine judge. It judges and consumes whatever persons, and whatever aspects of each person, have failed to rise to its own condition of fiery activity and bright unrestricted awareness. To some extent, indeed, everyone and everything, by hardening into its own selfhood, has failed to become a pure dancing spurt of flame, and thus stands under the judgment. To become flame or to become cinder is the inescapable and constant dilemma to which every moving being must and does make his small contributory response at every moment.

CHAPTER VI

MAN AMONG MEN

80. Thinking is common to all.

81. Men should speak with rational awareness and thereby hold on strongly to that which is shared in common—as a city holds on to its law, and even more strongly. For all human laws are nourished by the one divine law, which prevails as far as it wishes, suffices for all things, and yet is something more than they.

82. The people should fight for their law as for their city wall.

83. Law involves obeying the counsel of one.

84. To me one man is worth ten thousand if he is first-rate.

85. The best of men choose one thing in preference to all else, immortal glory in preference to mortal goods; whereas the masses simply glut themselves like cattle.

86. Gods and men honor those slain in battle.

87. Even he who is most in repute knows only what is reputed and holds fast to it.

88. To extinguish hybris is more needful than to extinguish a fire.

89. It is weariness to keep toiling at the same things so that one becomes ruled by them.

90. Dogs bark at a person whom they do not know.

91. What mental grasp, what sense have they? They believe the tales of the poets and follow the crowd as their teachers, ignoring the adage that the many are bad, the good are few.

92. Men are deceived in their knowledge of things that are manifest— even as Homer was, although he was the wisest of all Greeks. For he was even deceived by boys killing lice when they said to him: "What we have seen and grasped, these we leave behind; whereas what we have not seen and grasped, these we carry away."

93. Homer should be turned out of the lists and flogged, and Archilochus too.

94. Hesiod distinguishes between good days and evil days, not knowing that every day is like every other.

95. The Ephesians had better go hang themselves, every man of them, and leave their city to be governed by youngsters, for they have banished Hermadorus, the finest man among them, declaring: "Let us not have anyone amongst us who excels the rest; if there should be such a one, let him go and live elsewhere."

96. May you have plenty of wealth, you men of Ephesus, in order that you may be punished for your evil ways!

97. After birth men wish to live and accept their dooms; then they leave behind them children to become dooms in their turn.

UNLIKE Pythagoras, Heraclitus was not a founder of communities. His attitude toward community is forcefully ambivalent. In a profound sense the community is divine, and all human laws are nourished by the universal and all-sufficient divine law (Fr. 81), which is the intelligence that "steers all things through all things" (Fr. 120). On the other hand, any actual community is found to be made up largely of those moist and drunken souls that Heraclitus despises. To characterize the political aspect of Heraclitus' philosophy requires an equable recognition of these two opposing and mutually qualifying ideas.

Frs. 95 and 96 give brief indication of an event that doubtless had a sharp impact on the philosopher and confirmed him in his misanthropic cast of mind. Nothing is known about Hermadorus, nor about the grounds on which the Ephesians banished him; but there is no doubt concerning Heraclitus' judgment of the matter. And whatever personal chagrin and deprivation he may have felt at the banishment of a friend, it is evident that his thought must have been concerned with the more general political danger of which the incident was a reminder—the ever-present threat of collective mediocrity against the outstanding individual. Dogs, after all, bark at anyone whom they do not recognize (Fr. 90).

Mediocrity is given a more positive meaning in Fr. 88 through the concept of *hybris*. In the Introduction I have translated the word as "flagrant self-assertion," and the phrase can be retained, although some further connotations may be noted. The more usual translation by such words as "pride" and "arrogance," although not wrong, is perhaps more liable to misunderstanding. Heraclitus himself seems to have been a proud and even an arrogant man, if we may credit the persistent ancient stories about him. He is surely not saying that his own kind of pride should be extinguished. The passion of distance was especially strong in him, and the quality of soul that is spoken of in Fr. 88 has to be understood as something opposed and antagonistic to the proud aristocratic struggle toward the light. Accordingly both Burnet and Fairbanks have seen fit to translate *hybris* as "wantonness," and Fairbanks' version of the Fragment reads: "Wantonness must be quenched more than a conflagration." This, at any rate, indicates an indispensable part of the idea. What the word connotes is spiritual slackness and arrogance together: it is the slackness that takes satisfaction in being slack. In every soul there is a tendency to become spiritually loose, riotous, and in this sense egotistical, and the tendency must be mastered if there is to be integrity and upward growth in either the individual or the community. The prized condition of soul and society alike is a tautness like that of a cord of the bow drawn back, or like that of the strings of a properly tuned lyre (Fr. 117). A loosening of the bow's cord prevents the archer from hitting the bull's-eye; a loosening of the lyre's strings prevents the lyrist from producing musical sounds. *Hybris* is the loosening of one's inner cord, with the result that self-control is lost and the soul becomes moist and slovenly. Incidentally, there is a typical paradox in the fact that Heraclitus employs the simile of a conflagration when the condition of which he is speaking is, according to his usual metaphor, not a fiery but a watery one.

Still, in acknowledging the foregoing distinction it must be recalled that for Heraclitus there is always another and contrary side to every situation. *Hybris*, like everything else, is ambivalent, and can be seen in double perspective. While on the one hand it represents the "moist" and arrogant vanity that characterizes inferior souls, it has a more universal significance too. For there is a sense in which everything tends to persist in its own specific being, and in which every person strives to retain and assert his own selfhood. Self-assertion, even flagrant self-assertion, is a universal characteristic; it is what makes possible and inevitable the strife that gives a meaning to existence, and without which all things would cease to be (Fr. 27). On the human level it becomes more specifically egoistic; there, in dramatic perspective, it supplies the tragic flaw (ἁμαρτία) which Aristotle regarded as the efficient cause of authentic tragedy.[1] The central tragic insight, generalized beyond the boundaries of the stage, regards human self-assertion, which is to say human existence, as always in the long run self-terminating. Heraclitus would have agreed, but his agreement does not involve nihilism or melodrama or self-pity. For termination does not mean defeat, except for those who are its unwilling victims. The wise and serene soul, moving with confidence and grace toward the light, accepts the temporality and the conditions of it by his own choice (cf. Fr. 45); and thus he makes himself not a defeated victim of change but a participant in the divine process of self-overcoming.

Those who express and choose the better way, instead of slipping into the worse (granted that both ways are, in ultimate reckoning, necessary complementaries) are referred to in Frs. 84, 85, and 86. To die in battle—i.e., in a condition of intense activity—is far more honorable and excellent than to die in sluggish illness.[2] The first-rate man (ἄριστος) is a dry, active soul; he does not follow the crowd and their popular slogans (Fr. 91), and in a good community he would be the natural ruler (Fr. 84). But from the turgidity and confusion of actual communities he must lead his essential life apart, even as wisdom "stands apart from all else" (Fr. 7).

Yet, while there is a sense in which he must stand apart, there is also a sense in which the superior man must never fall into isolation: he must maintain, through quickened perceptions and intelligence, an active and ever renewed kinship with the fiery Logos that encompasses him. Such kinship cannot be realized entirely in isolation; it is necessary to be "guided by what is common" (Frs. 2, 15), while at the same time correcting and challenging men's false apprehensions of it. The importance of this principle of shared yet directed experience finds political embodiment in Fr. 81. The Fragment begins with a pun upon the Greek expressions for "in common" and "with rational awareness";[3] it then proceeds to introduce a word that has not appeared in any of the previous Fragments, but which is now employed in Frs. 81, 82, and 83—the word νόμος, law. Both Reinhardt and Gigon think that there is a distinction to be made between "all human laws" and "the laws of the city"—the former representing the customs, precepts, and traditions, in short the unwritten laws by which human life is largely carried on, while the latter are the codified laws. The distinction may seem to have some justification in the fact that the first translation of this word given by Liddell, Scott, and Jones is "that which is in habitual practice, use or possession." But while the word is there further said to mean "custom, usage," the more definite meaning is also given, "statute, ordinance made by authority." In any case, Kirk wisely rejects the distinction as misleading;[4] for the Greeks regarded the codified laws as growing out of and supported by the unwritten laws, and both of them are said by Heraclitus to participate, although imperfectly, in the "one divine law."

Although the one divine Nomos is not essentially different from the one divine Logos, there is a suggestive difference in connotation, determined by the difference of the metaphors that are represented. The doctrine that is brought in with the new word contains an indispensable part of the full truth—namely, that a community can thrive only if there is some mutuality of rational awareness among the citizens, and that such rational and communal awareness can come only by drawing upon the divine source.

The comparison in Fr. 82 between the law and the city wall is not accidental. The wall of a city in ancient times was far more than bricks and mortar; it was a kind of magical encirclement, representing and guaranteeing some kind of supernatural protection. Much later, in Vergil's *Aeneid*, there are two oblique but suggestive references to the importance of the city wall. The better known of them involves the episode of the wooden horse, filled with Greek warriors, which by treachery gained entrance into the walls of Troy and led to the city's downfall. It seems unlikely that in actual fact the Trojans would have been deceived by so gross and strange a maneuver, and the real question comes to be how such a fantastic story might have arisen. The legend could well have grown out of the exaggerated emphasis laid upon the protective power of the city wall, with the resulting sense that the safety and autonomy of the city are lost when this protective encirclement has been violated. The other Vergilian reference occurs in the account of how Queen Dido won by a stratagem her right to build a kingdom in North Africa. A local potentate named Byrsa jokingly granted her as much land as could be encompassed by a bull's hide, and Dido met the condition by having her men cut the hide into very thin strips, whereby a considerable area could be encompassed, on which to build the city of Carthage. It is impossible to trace the origin of the playful legend; and the fact that *byrsa* is the Greek word for bull's hide proves nothing, because the name of an anonymous North African could have been invented to suit the story.[5] But the bull was a sacred animal to worshipers of Dionysus and of Mithra, perhaps also to some other sects, and it was likely enough that the bull might have become associated with the divine power guarding the boundaries of a city. Nothing is proved by the two Vergilian episodes, except that they seem to add to the evidence of how dearly the ancient peoples regarded their city wall. What Heraclitus is doing in Frs. 82 and 81 is to connect the idea of the city wall with that of the city's law, and to connect the city's law (including what is unwritten) with "sharing in common" and, by the help of the pun, with "rational awareness."

The remaining Fragments of the group do not require special comment. Fr. 97 brings the group to a close on a note of somberness—not a gratuitous pessimism, but a naturally resultant expression of Heraclitus' general philosophy. The first clause states something rather close to the Freudian doctrine of the death-wish: that even at birth we accept, in an unconscious layer of the mind, the fact of coming death. Still we push on, in spite of the dark recognition, and we think we strive toward the light although darkness is no less a real part of our unconscious attachment. Moreover, along with the open will to survive and the hidden attachment to death, there is also the urgency to reproduce, and the expression of it leads to a renewal of the problem and the paradox in our offspring. A frank, clear awareness of mankind's common destiny and doom is what marks alike the philosophy of Heraclitus and the crucial moments in the greatest Greek tragedies.

CHAPTER VII

RELATIVITY AND PARADOX

98. Opposition brings concord. Out of discord comes the fairest harmony.

99. It is by disease that health is pleasant; by evil that good is pleasant; by hunger, satiety; by weariness, rest.

100. Men would not have known the name of justice if these things had not occurred.

101. Sea water is at once very pure and very foul: it is drinkable and healthful for fishes, but undrinkable and deadly for men.

102. Donkeys would prefer straw to gold.

103. Pigs wash in mud, and domestic fowls in dust or ashes.

104. The handsomest ape is ugly compared with humankind; the wisest man appears as an ape when compared with a god—in wisdom, in beauty, and in all other ways.

105. A man is regarded as childish by a spirit, just as a boy is by a man.

106. To God all things are beautiful, good, and right; men, on the other hand, deem some things right and others wrong.

107. Doctors cut, burn, and torture the sick, and then demand of them an undeserved fee for such services.

108. The way up and the way down are one and the same.

109. In the circle the beginning and the end are common.

110. Into the same rivers we step and we do not step.

111. For wool-carders the straight way and the winding way are one and the same.

112. The bones connected by joints are at once a unitary whole and not a unitary whole. To be in agreement is to differ; the concordant is the discordant. From out of all the many particulars comes oneness, and out of oneness come all the many particulars.

113. It is one and the same thing to be living or dead, awake or asleep, young or old. The former aspect in each case becomes the latter, and the latter again the former, by sudden unexpected reversal.

114. Hesiod, whom so many accept as their wise teacher, did not even understand the nature of day and night; for they are one.

115. The name of the bow is life, but its work is death.

AN INTELLECTUAL ALERTNESS, which is so essential a characteristic, to Heraclitus, both of the cosmic fiery light and of the individual intelligence that strives to become like it, is also demanded of anyone who would read Heraclitus' chiseled remarks with understanding. A reader who falls into static interpretations and stereotyped associations will miss a part of the meaning of almost every utterance. Man learns to exercise his mind by shaping his experiences—perceived, remembered, and imagined—into concepts, and this is a useful and clarifying procedure so far as it goes; but then as a kind of mental safety-play he tends to regard his network of concepts as equivalent to truth itself, and thus he disposes himself to shut out of serious consideration any intuitive possibilities that do not have a fixable relation to the conceptual system (cf. Fr. 63). Heraclitus challenges our customary concepts and our customary methods of forming and relating concepts by a sometimes startling use of what Asclepius calls his "symbolical and gymnastical" style of thinking and writing.[1]

The most characteristic difficulty in Heraclitus' philosophy lies in the demand which it makes upon its hearers to transcend the "either-or" type of thinking and to recognize in each phase of experience that a relationship of "both-and" may be present in subtle ways that escape a dulled intelligence. Heraclitus' thought moves not by exclusion but more characteristically by coalescence, and always with a sense of otherness. To him nothing is exclusively this or that; in various ways he affirms something to be *both* of two disparates or two contraries, leaving the reader to contemplate the paradox, the full semantic possibilities of which can never be exhausted by plain prose statements. The upward and downward ways are contrary and yet one; the human soul is destined and yet is faced with the ever-present choice between up and down; the soul originates out of fire (Fr. 28) but it originates out of water (Fr. 44); time is eternal and yet time, like everything else, must come to a death which is also a rebirth; God is at once universal process, the intelligence that steers the process, the model by which a wise man will guide himself (Fr. 106), and a child idly moving counters in a game. To be sure, the logicizing intellect will undertake to analyze each of these paradoxes into its elements, explaining in just what pair of respects, or in what pair of circumstances, or from what opposite points of view, something is at once such and not-such. But Heraclitus regards the paradox itself, and not its logical transformation, as more truly representing the real state of affairs.

It is this acceptance of the ontological status of paradox— an acceptance, that is to say, of the view that paradox lies inextricably at the very heart of reality—that gave Heraclitus his ancient reputation for obscurity; and it is what stamps his philosophy with a different quality from that of an Ionian scientist such as Anaximander, or even from that of an Eleatic or a Pythagorean. To be sure, gnomic utterances were nothing new. The sense of the cryptic was strongly marked in the rising poetic consciousness of the sixth century B.C. Philosophers, however, were expected to be able to catch a glimpse of something steadier and more permanent. It was gradually coming to be recognized that their task was to look for the ἀρχή (the fundamental principle of things, which is also their beginning) and the λόγος (the fundamental principle, which is also the meaning that can be uttered or that comes to the receptively wise man as if divinely uttered to him), and that these would somehow explain the manifold and fluctuating particulars. The earlier scientific philosophers of Miletus, Thales, and his followers, had sought a principle amid the elements of the physical world; although the most speculative of them, Anaximander, pushed his imagination farther and attained to a transcendental notion—the idea of an infinite "Boundless," from which all physical manifestations come into existence and back into which they vanish. Pythagoreans and Eleatics, with different orientations, explored the farther reaches of transcendental method—an exploration that Plato was later to pursue with an unexampled many-sidedness of imaginative approach. The peculiar difference that marks the Fragments of Heraclitus grows out of his refusal to accept either of these two recognized types of explanation. Although his philosophy shows a certain resemblance to both the naturalistic and the transcendental philosophy in particular respects, he is not content to take either a perceptible physical substance or a postulated metaphysical entity as the be-all of existence. As remarked in Chapter III, the fire of which he speaks is neither strictly physical nor strictly metaphysical; it is physical and metaphysical together; for it is the feeding flame, perceptible both to outward sight and as inward exuberance, and at the same time it is the universal fact of perpetual change. The concrete and the absolute meanings of it overlap, and consequently no such clear-cut doctrine as the view of Thales that everything is water, or the atomic theory that was to come with Leucippus and Democritus, or an Eleatic definition of real being as timeless, can ever emerge in him. Heraclitus is unwilling to pursue clarity at the cost of distorting the truth of things as he finds it in the confused, shifting, and paradoxical manifestations throughout experience. It is the bold attempt to put this elusive character of truth into some kind of nearly adequate language that gives to the Fragments their characteristic temper and characteristic difference which caused their author to be called "the dark one."

As an introduction to the more pointedly paradoxical statements that follow (Frs. 108ff.) a glance may be given to Frs. 98-107, which record somewhat more commonplace observations about the relativity of perceptual and valuational judgments. Such statements of experiential relativity do contain seeds of paradox to be sure, but actually they do no more than set certain conditions upon which possibilities of opposing points of view may rest. The development of such opposition into the succinct semantic tension that is paradox comes about when a way is found of declaring the opposing terms to be not only mutually related, but somehow identical. It can easily be observed how this has been done in a variety of ways in Frs. 108-115, whereas the earlier Fragments offer more explicit comparison of various pairs of opposites, stating either their causal or epistemological involvement with each other or their axiological relativity.

In the case of a writer like Heraclitus, who employs figures of speech not for prettification but as a means of exploring and adumbrating some of the more hidden aspects of reality, it is helpful to examine the ways in which those figures of speech function semantically; and one of the most indicative questions of this sort has to do with the way in which paradox and metaphor are related. For each of these two tropes tends to involve the other whenever it is employed seriously and not superficially. By "superficial" and "serious" I mean what I have elsewhere designated by the words "surface" and "depth."[2] There is both a paradox of surface and a paradox of depth, and there is both a metaphor of surface and a metaphor of depth. A surface paradox is correctly defined as a "seeming contradiction"; it can be explained away by making the proper logical qualifications. A surface metaphor is a tabloid simile; it declares in effect that something is like something else, but it does this more briefly by dropping out the word "like" and saying that the something *is* the something else. Depth paradox and depth metaphor, on the other hand, always tend to occur somehow in mutual association. In the most characteristic utterances of Heraclitus, in particular, paradox and metaphor show something of this mutuality; with the result that his paradoxes and his metaphors are essential, not superficial—*you cannot unsay them.* You can unsay a paradox such as "Christ was not a Christian" or "Freud was not a Freudian": you can explain it away by remarking that Christ or Freud would not have identified himself with the views or practices of his self-professed followers. Again, you can unsay a metaphor such as "He is a fox"; for this is but an abbreviation of the simile, "He is as crafty as a fox." When, on the other hand, Heraclitus speaks about the cosmic fire, it is impossible to drop the figurative language without essential loss; the relation between semantic vehicle and semantic tenor is organic, not mechanical. And when he declares a basic paradox, such as the identity of the upward and downward ways, it is not possible to explain this entirely away by a reshuffling and redefinition of logical components.

In short, if metaphor and paradox are to serve a metaphysical purpose, each must to some degree involve the other. If metaphor is employed without a touch of paradox, it loses its radically metaphoric character and turns out to be virtually no more than a tabloid simile. If paradox is employed without metaphor, it is no more than a witticism or sophism. The double principle is so important for understanding Heraclitus' more obscure Fragments that it is worth while to look at each of the two complementary aspects separately.

(I) First, then, metaphor, if it is semantic rather than merely grammatical, involves paradox. A merely grammatical metaphor is one that could be restated as a simile without essential loss—that is, without semantic alteration, without distortion of meaning. To call a man a pig is to say in effect, "He eats like a pig"; and in changing the sentence from "He is a pig" to "He eats like a pig" there is no appreciable change of meaning. The simile sets in explicit relation the two elements of discourse, *man* and *pig*, which even in the metaphoric version the speaker must really have kept distinct and unconfused in his mind. He could do this because he knew, independently of the specific attempt to connect them, what a man is and what a pig is. Hence the metaphor in such a case differs from the corresponding simile in hardly more than a verbal way; the difference is but one of grammatical formulation.

Consider, by contrast, any of the metaphors by which Heraclitus or any other philosopher attempts to characterize the fundamental reality: that it is an ever-living fire (Fr. 29), that it is wisdom (Fr. 119) or intelligence (Fr. 120) or reason (Frs. 1, 2, 118), or (passing quite beyond the Heraclitean context) that it is love. A metaphoric assertion of such a kind cannot be reduced to a simile without a subtle change creeping into the meaning. Suppose that instead of saying, "God is reason," one were to say, "God is *like* reason." Although there is an apparent gain in logical precision here, the appearance of clarity is misleading, for a certain unspoken assumption has been unwittingly introduced. In uttering the simile we assume that we know independently what God is and what reason is, and that it is possible to discover a relation of similarity between the two ideas independently conceived. In our previous example, of calling a man a pig, the condition is adequately met. We know by independent sets of experiences what a man is and what a pig is; we are then able to say that in a particular instance we can discover in what is undeniably a man certain specific similarities to what can be independently recognized as a pig. The situation is mainly one of comparison, and that is why it is possible to restate the apparent metaphor, "He is a pig," in the form of a simile, "He eats like a pig." Here, obviously, it is the simile, not the metaphor, that expresses more exactly what is meant.

But in the three metaphysical metaphors just cited no parallel situation is present. The subject-term—whether we use the word "It" or "God" or "Reality" or whatever else—is not known independently of the three predicates that are successively attached to it. One does not first know the Ultimate and then find that it bears a certain similarity to intelligence, to fire, to love, etc. Such imperfect knowledge as we can have of the Ultimate is had *through* such attributes, by attending to the overreach of meaning that each of them can suggest, beyond the trade-meanings of ordinary experience. As a perceptive man stumbles along on his pilgrimage through experience he discovers that some qualities and some relationships are semantically more promising than others, in that they tend to suggest fuller meanings than lie on the surface or than are grasped on early acquaintance. The serious percipient finds himself led on, then (partly but not exclusively influenced by conditioning factors from outside), to regard certain aspects of his world as divine; and he may attempt to verbalize his insights by such metaphors as "God is the bright sky" or "God is fire," or at a more developed stage, "God is intelligence" or "God is love." But each of these metaphors, whether it grows out of primitive or more matured experience, is a paradox. To identify the ultimate Reality with some finite part of itself is to say, in effect, "The Infinite is the finite." Yet in speaking of Divinity a use of radical metaphor is unavoidable. Such metaphor must always be radical, not merely grammatical; which is to say, it must work mainly not by comparison, like a simile, but by insight and transcendental probing. To say that fire or wisdom or love is divine is to start with one of these three specific and familiar phenomena and to become reverently open, attentive, and responsive to the values and suggestions of transcendental association that may, without looseness or irresponsibility, be found in it. In pursuing this eductive course—this semantic passage from the more everyday and familiar to the darkly hinted at—we employ a metaphor which by literal standards says too much. We declare, "Fire is divine," or we turn the sentence around and declare, "God is fire." And the result, in either direction—if the implications of the transcendental term are not ignored or caricatured—is flagrantly paradoxical.

(II) But if serious metaphor thus involves paradox, it is also conversely true that serious paradox involves metaphor. This converse involvement can be shown by examining paradox in the same double manner in which we have examined metaphor—looking first at ordinary, superficial paradox and then observing how radical paradox differs from it. Now ordinary paradox, or paradox of surface, as has been said, is merely a trick of speech whereby a point can be made more wittily and effectively. "Christ was no Christian," "Freud was no Freudian," "Nothing is more fatiguing than leisure," or Chesterton's "Nothing is so miraculous as the commonplace," etc.—such paradoxes as these may grace an evening's conversation and give the perpetrator a reputation for cleverness, but actually they depend for their effect upon a more or less deliberate confusion between two connotations of a word—e.g., between Christianity as it is practiced and Christianity defined as adhering to the principles of its founder, or between genuine leisure and the sheer inoccupancy in which one burdens oneself with trifles, or between the dramatic sort of miracle that involves a breaking away from the commonplace and the ultimate metaphysical miracle that existence and order should be instead of nonexistence or chaos.

By contrast, a radical and serious paradox does not hang upon a removable confusion, but is demanded by the complexity and inherent ambiguity of what is being expressed. Fr. 108, one of the most familiar sayings of Heraclitus, offers an example. To say that the way up and the way down are one and the same is, if taken literally, false and absurd; such a statement is not even a paradox, but merely a piece of nonsense. Yet it is evident that Heraclitus was attempting to declare something deeply significant here. How is it possible to understand the identification as making sense rather than nonsense? Obviously, as every reader immediately perceives, the statement must be taken metaphorically. Paradox implies metaphor, in that the upward way can be identified with the downward way only with respect to certain metaphoric connotations of each. Now in Heraclitean context the upward way is the way from earth to water to fire, and the downward way is the reverse. But these two directions of transformation

[98]

occur not only in physical nature but also in the life of the self. Moreover, the phrase "one and the same" must also be interpreted with some metaphoric flexibility: it evidently, means to say that the two contrary processes are both going-on all the time, and that their continual and varying tension is what makes existence and life possible. Thus a meaningful interpretation of the paradox in Fr. 108 serves to reveal several metaphors that are latent in it. And in general, with differences in detail, much the same thing will be found to be true in all of Heraclitus' paradoxes.

The question of the use of figurative language comes up in a rather special respect in Fr. 111, "For wool-carders the straight way and the winding way are the same." Naturally, the literal meaning of a passage should be established first, in order to avoid ill-grounded inferences as to the symbolical tenor. Hippolytus, when quoting the present Fragment in *The Refutation of All Heresies*, explains the literal situation thus: "The circular movement of an instrument in the fuller's shop called 'the screw' is at once straight and curved, in that it revolves upwards and circularly at the same time."[3] If this were the double motion that Heraclitus had had in mind, a simultaneity of a straight and a curved propulsion, as a pair of component movements, it would not be easy to see just what symbolic reference might have been intended. Heraclitus, however, shows no evidence of possessing a developed geometrical imagination, and would probably not have thought in terms of component movements. Moreover, the instrument called "the screw," although it evidently was employed by fullers at the time when Hippolytus wrote, probably had not been invented seven centuries earlier in Heraclitus' day. Then, too, it should be noted that the word σκολιός means not only "curved" but also, and more loosely, "winding, twisted, tangled." All in all, although it is not certain just what process of wool-carding was current in the earlier period, it seems probable that the meaning of the Fragment depends in part upon a pun in the word for "straight," which in Greek carried a moral connotation, "right" or "straight-forward," as well as the geometrical one. On one level of its meaning, then, the Fragment could be taken to say, "For wool-carders the right way (i.e., for them as craftsmen) is the winding way." But then, just as one paradox emerges from taking the first adjective to mean "straight," so another paradox also emerges from the moral overtones of the second adjective, which can mean not only "winding" but also "un-righteous, unjust, deceptive." Heraclitus employs a word-play of this kind with serious intent, for to his mind the occasional duplicity of language has an intimate connection with, and reveals, the duplicity and paradoxicality of the thing referred to.

Another Fragment in the group—Fr. 115, "The name of the bow is life, but its work is death"—also depends upon a pun to make its point. One of the two Greek words for "bow" is βιός with the accent on the final syllable, whereas one of the two main words for life is βίος with the accent on the initial syllable. The linguistic accident, whereby a death-dealing in-strument has a name so similar to a word for life, seems to Heraclitus to be significantly related to the great paradoxical fact that life and death are but two intertwining aspects of the same thing, both of them being present and producing an ever-changing tension in every phenomenon.

Finally there is the compact group of expressive ambigui-ties in Fr. 109, "In the circle, the beginning and the end are common." All four terms need to be examined here. The least important of them, although not to be overlooked, is the suggestion of a pun which the word ξυνός always appears to carry for Heraclitus—an interplay of the two meanings, "in common" and "with understanding" (cf. Note to Fr. 81). The ideas of "the end which is also a beginning" and the "be-ginning which is also an end" are a pair of archetypal para-doxes that have had a wide appeal to thoughtful men. One set of connotations is temporal, suggesting two ways, a forward and a backward, of looking at the passage of time. In spatial representation their precarious truth is manifested most clearly in the geometrical figure of the circle. Most important of all, there is the deeper symbolic sense in which beginning and end are, or can be and should be, related. A philosopher slightly later than Heraclitus, Alcmaeon of Crotona, expresses this further meaning in his remark, "Men perish because they cannot join the beginning with the end."[4] Alcmaeon's words for beginning and end are ἀρχή and τέλος; the former of which connotes also "first principle," the latter "governing aim." Heraclitus also says ἀρχή, but his word πέρας, signifying end in the sense of limit or boundary, does not in itself carry the second additional connotation. Nevertheless, it receives something of the fuller symbolic meaning from the connotations of the other words in the sentence, as well as from the realistic awareness, so characteristic of the ancient Greeks, that the idea of limit is always especially pertinent to human affairs. The overtones of the word "circle" are widely shared in different ages and different cultures; for here a geometrical figure is immediately presented to the imagination, independently of any special linguistic usage. In many an ancient culture the idea of the circle could mean at once the spatial figure, a cycle of events in time, and that serene condition of affairs in which there is regularity of movement about a still central point, whereby the initiating principle of life and its guiding end are brought into harmonious union.

CHAPTER VIII

THE HIDDEN HARMONY

116. The hidden harmony is better than the obvious.

117. People do not understand how that which is at variance with itself agrees with itself. There is a harmony in the bending back, as in the case of the bow and the lyre.

118. Listening not to me but to the Logos, it is wise to acknowledge that all things are one.

119. Wisdom is one and unique; it is unwilling and yet willing to be called by the name of Zeus.

120. Wisdom is one—to know the intelligence by which all things are steered through all things.

121. God is day and night, winter and summer, war and peace, satiety and want. But he undergoes transformations, just as *****, when it is mixed with a fragrance, is named according to the particular savor [that is introduced].

122. The sun will not overstep his measures; if he were to do so, the Erinyes, handmaids of justice, would seek him out.

123. All things come in their due seasons.

124. Even sleepers are workers and collaborators in what goes on in the universe.

So CLOSELY has Heraclitus' name been associated in Western philosophical tradition with the related themes of change and paradox, that there has often been a tendency to overlook the peculiar emphasis which he gives to the unity, in a qualified and paradoxical sense, of all things. Writers on ancient philosophy have sometimes been tempted to schematize their material by contrasting Parmenides and Heraclitus as representing extreme opposite tendencies, thereby producing a vast philosophical conundrum which the so-called "later naturalists"—Empedocles, Anaxagoras, Leucippus and Democritus

—undertook to solve by their diversely ingenious types of metaphysical integration. Of course there is a large half-truth in this way of envisaging the matter: for it cannot be denied that Parmenides is above all else the philosopher of unity and permanence, who regards every apparent evidence of variety or change as *ipso facto* illusory; nor can it be denied that Heraclitus accepts variety and change as basic and inexpungeable facts about the real nature of things. Unquestionably the opposition between the philosophers is there for all to see. Nevertheless, the resulting stereotype, which represents them as doctrinally contrasted and nothing more, can be grossly overdone. Relatively few qualifications need to be made for Parmenides, no doubt; but the philosophy of Heraclitus is too subtle, manifold, and shifting to be defined in such static terms. Granted that variety and change constitute a main theme, perhaps even *the* main theme for Heraclitus, there is nevertheless a second theme, running contrapuntally throughout the doctrine, which is equally indispensable—the theme expressed most plainly in Fr. 118, that "all things are one." It is misleading to call Heraclitus a pluralist without adding that he is somehow a monist as well, or to stress his doctrine of change, chance, and strife without adding that these characteristics, real and basic though they are, exist somehow counterbalanced by a tendency toward order, pattern, and harmony, which is equally inherent in what we must call (knowing that words fail us here) reality.

Still, the mode of balancing requires careful attention and careful statement. The peculiar sense in which Heraclitus accepts cosmic oneness as a reality cannot be indicated by any of the usual philosophical labels. Even so learned a Heraclitean scholar as Hermann Diels made the mistake, some fifteen years after compiling his valuable collection of the Fragments, of putting forward an interpretation of Heraclitus as a metaphysical dualist. In his article on the philosopher in Hastings' *Encyclopaedia of Religion and Ethics* Diels espouses a distinction between what he calls the "husk" and the "kernel" of Heraclitus' doctrine—the former term referring to the fiery world of change, the latter to the ultimate oneness of the Logos. He even goes so far as to support his quasi-Platonic interpretation by some apparently biased translation. For example, Fr. 120 ends with the phrase, πάντα διὰ πάντων, which characterizes the cosmic intelligence as steering "all things through all things"—an idea of typical Heraclitean complexity; Diels, however, changes his translation in the Encylopaedia article to read, "which knows and governs all things." Now there is a good deal of connotative difference between this phrase and the one that Heraclitus uses, and the difference becomes even more significant when it is realized that the verb which I have translated "are steered" (to avoid an excessive suggestion of individual liberty) might equally well, or almost equally well, be translated "steer themselves." For the difference between the Greek passive and the Greek middle voice is not grammatically indicated in certain tenses, and a number of Heraclitus' phrases suggest an inseparable coalescence of the two kinds of idea. The intelligence—which is also to say the thunderbolt (Fr. 35)—that does the steering operates on particular things, including human individuals, from within as well as from without; and the result, as several earlier chapters have shown in different perspectives, is a universe in which unity, diversity, self-direction, chance, and ambiguity all commingle. But Diels' mistranslation enables him to reach the strange and unacceptable conclusion that "Heraclitus comprehends, as exactly as his opponent Parmenides, who only partly understood him, noumena and phenomena, truth and illusion, in his system."[1] It is one thing to compare, another to equalize, such diverse thinkers as Heraclitus and Parmenides. The kinds of cosmic unity for which they respectively stand are radically different.

Diels' dualistic interpretation of Heraclitus causes him to belittle such statements as Fr. 24 ("Time is a child moving counters in a game") and Fr. 40 ("The fairest universe is but a heap of rubbish piled up at random") as referring only to "ephemeral experience," which he thinks represents to Heraclitus "the mutable, inconsistent, unconscious, and childish world of change." But to Heraclitus' notion *all* experience is ephemeral, and *all*-things are mutable and partly or potentially inconsistent. Diels, however, connects Frs. 24 and 40 with Heraclitus' denunciation of polymathy (Fr. 6), and he opposes the three Fragments as a group to the statements that "wisdom stands apart from all else" (Fr. 7) and that self-knowledge is needful as the way of wisdom (Frs. 8, 9). Now it is true that Heraclitus is against polymathy, or mere extensive learning for its own sake, and that he regards the way of wisdom as lying through self-knowledge, or at least as inseparable from it. In Fragments 6 and 9 he is asking the important question, "What is the best way of thinking?" or, "In what does an intellectually superior attitude toward the universe consist?" And the answer which he affirms is quite different from that which Diels attributes to him. For while wisdom is "apart" from other things, in the sense that it is intrinsically more valuable than they, such wisdom is genuine only if it is a fiery activity, able to reflect the changing facets of the world itself—"for the moving world can only be known by what is in motion" (Fr. 43).

The unity of things as Heraclitus understands it is a subtle and hidden sort of unity, not at all such as could be expressed by either a monistic or a dualistic philosophy. The oneness of things, or rather their mutual attunement, cannot exist or even be conceived apart from their manyness and discord. The wisdom that steers all things through all things (overtone: "the wisdom by which all things steer themselves through all things") is something that cannot be expressed without paradox. To call it "God" or "Zeus" is at once necessary and misleading (Fr. 119). It is necessary, because there is no way in which to refer to or think about the ultimate cosmological problem of the relatedness of all things except by employing the least inadequate symbols that we possess. On the other hand, any divine name is misleading, because of the doctrinal and mythological associations that it almost inevitably conjures up in people's minds. No attempt to characterize the ultimate unity of things, or the power and tendency toward unity, can possibly succeed, and yet man's inquiring mind cannot permanently abandon the attempt.

The transcendent neutrality of ultimate reality is indicated in Fr. 121, where unfortunately a crucial word, here indicated by asterisks, is missing in the extant manuscript of Hippolytus—presumably dropped out accidentally by a copyist. Certain scholars, including Diels and Burnet, have arbitrarily guessed that the missing word was "fire," but there is no textual support for this, and I cannot see in it anything more than a sort of scholarly stock response: "Heraclitus, ergo fire." Moreover, there is no custom on record, so far as I am aware, either among the ancient Greeks or anywhere else, of naming fire according to the incense (or possibly, as some translators have it, the spices) that are thrown into it. A more plausible suggestion has been put forward by Hermann Fränkel,[2] who suggests that the missing word might have referred to the pure oily base with which different perfumes were blended in making ointments, which would then be called by one name or another according to the resultant savor. The oily base (or possibly beeswax?) that was employed in such manufacture would of course have to be entirely pure, in the sense of not possessing any odor in itself. Consequently the point of the comparison would be (if Fränkel's theory is right) that the ultimate reality (what can be called, and yet cannot be called, God or Zeus) is itself so pure and unparticularized that it does not possess any qualities whatever, thus being susceptible to any and all manifestations and changes.

But can nothing more definite about the cosmic World-All be said? To regard it as having no characteristics, being no

sort of *this* as distinguished from *that*, is to reduce it to a
virtual semantic zero. And yet Heraclitus is quite evidently
endeavoring to say something, and he evidently attaches
meaning to what he wants to say. Is there any way, then,
in which ultimate reality can be characterized? What—to
put the question as provokingly as possible—can be uttered
about the Unutterable? One can only reply that while there
are indications, the indications are scattered and sometimes
in tensive opposition to one another, and that it would be
a mistake to pursue any of them too far or in exclusion.
There are indications of a kind of order, balance, and self-
steering in the universe (Frs. 29, 35, 120, 122), which, although it never halts the changing passage of time, does give
some kind of boundaries and character to universal change,
so that to the discerning mind the change is never simply
chaos. There are indications of a wisdom, intelligence, and
reason (Logos)—not to be measured and judged by the
petty and partisan standards of our human thought, but still
profoundly real and effective (Frs. 1, 2, 118, 119, 120).
And in the first two Fragments of the present chapter there
are indications of a cosmic order under the aspect of harmony.

Although it may possibly be true, as Kirk declares, that
the Greek word ἁρμονία did not acquire a musical meaning
until the latter part of the fifth century, the point seems to
be impossible to prove, and in any case Heraclitus would
still be introducing a musical analogy in his reference to the
lyre in Fr. 117. Already Pythagoras had taken the idea of
musical harmony (connoting in Greek music probably not
so much togetherness of sounds as a pleasing and fitting
array of sounds) as the central symbol of his doctrine; and
when discussing this doctrine with later Pythagoreans Socrates employs the word ἁρμονία.[3] So all in all I think it
is more justifiable to follow Fairbanks, Lattimore, and Kathleen Freeman in translating ἁρμονία as "harmony" than
to accept Burnet's word "attunement" or Kirk's word "con-

nexion." Heraclitus may perhaps be regarded as having taken the Pythagorean idea of harmony and added to it an observation of his own. Harmony, he adds, can exist only where there is contrast. There is no harmony of a single note, there is significant harmony only where there are "opposing tones" which are resolved.[4] Musical harmony involves the overcoming, but without the eliminating, of some musical opposition. And in the larger sphere of human existence the same situation is found to occur. Harmonies and attunements between person and person, or between person and circumstance, are brought into existence out of diversity and potential strife.

Moreover, there is not merely the contrariety of different musical notes, there is also a contrariety of tensions in the way in which the musical sound is produced. The strings of the lyre must be bent back and released, in order for the sound to come forth. Somewhat analogous, as Fr. 117 suggests, is the case of the bow. Pfleiderer sees in the conjunction of these two similes a reflection of the familiar Heraclitean paradox of life and death, and accordingly of the upward and downward ways.[5] But the Fragment shows no intention of making a comparison between the bow and the lyre; the comparison is rather between each of these instruments and the tenor of the argument. Looking at the double simile in this way we can see more fully what the tenor is. In the case of both the bow and the lyre a string has to be pulled back and strained in order to be released: that is evidently the simple fact on which the point of the Fragment rests. But what is the result, in the two cases, of releasing the string? In the one case there is a hitting of the mark, in the other a production of musical sound. The connection of these two ideas, when each of them is taken metaphorically, is a basic Pythagorean theme, and it is one which was congenial to Greek ethical thought generally. A missing of the mark (ἁμαρτία) is, according to Aristotle, the central flaw that precipitates tragedy;[6] and a human life to which the metaphor may justly be applied is also one that has fallen into disharmony—with other persons, with situations, and above all with itself, which is to say with its vocation. Contrariwise, the man who can hear and whose soul can echo "the music of the spheres" (as Pythagoras expressed his highest cosmological conception) is best equipped and readiest to know and recognize the truth. The idea implicit in the connection of bow and lyre, then, is presumably Pythagorean, or at least bears a striking resemblance to one of the highest tenets of Pythagoreanism; but the "bending back" represents Heraclitus' own distinctive emphasis.

The closing Fragment, Fr. 124, suggests a kind of resolution to the strongly tensive philosophy. Although it is better to be awake and to strive toward the light, yet even those who sleep and fall into darkness are still "workers and collaborators in what goes on in the universe." The idea is a favorite one with Stoic philosophers, and in fact it is Marcus Aurelius who has preserved the present Fragment by quoting it in his *Meditations*.[7] It is another expression of the paradox of the double perspective—ethical and cosmological—that is so central to Heraclitus and the Stoic alike. In ethical perspective the choice between the two ways lies before each of us, and to the alert mind it is an urgent choice; but in metaphysical perspective the upward and downward ways are both in process all the time, and all things eventually steer themselves numberless times in both directions; so that, in Heraclitus' inaccurate but succinct phrase, the two ways are "one and the same." It is better to be a man of calm wisdom than a fluttering fool, and better for one's intelligence to be dry and bright than to be a victim of moist emotions; nevertheless the foolish and the dissolute have their roles to play in the ever shifting universe, like everything else. The ultimate order of things is perfectly comprehensive and perfectly impartial; the countless individual particularities, each with its partisan aims and partisan point of view, become of infinitesimal significance in their relation to the whole. Every theory about the ultimate order, every attempt to make a statement about it, is bound to express one of those partisan and partial points of view; from which it follows that no theory of or statement about the cosmic wisdom, "by which all things are steered through all things," can ever do justice to the complexity and subtlety of that cosmic order itself. Even the word "wisdom" is a somewhat hapless metaphor as applied to it. Heraclitus would have been in agreement, could he have known it, with the opening remark of the *Tao Teh Ching*: "The *tao* that can be understood is not the real *tao*." The ultimate reality, of which Heraclitus is trying to speak, cannot be adequately represented either by a rationalistic concept such as "being" or "truth," or by a theological concept such as "Zeus" or "God," or by a naturalistic concept such as "fire" or "atoms." No word or image or idea can do it justice; but one of the least inadequate ways of symbolizing it, indicating as it does both its interrelating power and its elusiveness, is the phrase that Heraclitus employs in Fr. 116—*the hidden harmony.*

APPENDICES

In the following appendices the references to books and authors are usually designated by the surnames of their authors or editors. The one exception is *Doxographi Graeci*, edited by Hermann Diels, which is called "*Dox.*" to distinguish it from Diels' *Die Fragmente der Vorsokratiker*. The fourth edition of *Die Fragmente* (1920) is called "Diels" and the fifth edition (1934), as revised by Walter Kranz, is called "Diels-Kranz." Bibliographical details for all books cited in the notes will be found in Appendix B.

CONCORDANCE OF FRAGMENT NUMBERINGS
D-K = DIELS-KRANZ; BY = BYWATER

W	D-K	By	W	D-K	By	W	D-K	By
1	1	2	43	—	—	85	29	111
2	2	92	44	12	42	86	24	102
3	35	49	45	115	—	87	28	118
4	22	8	46	118	75	88	43	103
5	47	48	47	77	72	89	84b	82
6	40	16	48	117	73	90	97	115
7	108	18	49	36	68	91	104	111
8	101	80	50	125	84	92	56	—
9	116	106	51	85	105	93	42	119
10	112	107	52	110	104	94	106	120
11	55	13	53	95	108	95	121	114
12	101a	15	54	87	117	96	125a	—
13	107	4	55	34	3	97	20	86
14	73	94	56	46	132	98	8	46
15	89	95	57	17	5	99	111	104
16	21	64	58	7	37	100	23	60
17	123	10	59	98	38	101	61	52
18	93	11	60	96	85	102	9	51
19	18	7	61	78	96	103	37	53
20	—	—	62	—	—	104	82, 83	99, 98
21	91, 12	41	63	86	116	105	79	97
22	126	39	64	72	93	106	102	61
23	84a	83	65	26	77	107	58	58
24	52	79	66	62	67	108	60	69
25	53	24	67	27	122	109	103	70
26	80	62	68	63	123	110	49a	81
27	—	43	69	119	121	111	59	50
28	90	22	70	25	101	112	10	59
29	30	20	71	28	118	113	88	78
30	65	24	72	66	26	114	57	35
31	91	40	73	16	27	115	48	66
32	31	21	74	—	—	116	54	47
33	31	23	75	5	126	117	51	45
34	76	25	76	14	124, 125	118	50	1
35	64	28	77	15	127	119	32	65
36	6	32	78	5	130	120	41	19
37	3	—	79	92	12	121	67	36
38	99	31	80	113	91	122	94	29
39	120	30	81	114	91	123	100	34
40	124	—	82	44	100	124	75	90
41	11	55	83	33	110			
42	45	71	84	49	113			

APPENDIX A

NOTES TO CHAPTERS

INTRODUCTION

1. Plato *Laws* IV, 715 E; quoted by Diels-Kranz as fr. 6 under "Orpheus": ἀρχήν τε καὶ τελευτὴν καὶ μέσα τῶν ὄντων ἁπάντων ἔχων.

2. Strabo the geographer (XIV. i. 25) speaks of Thales as the first who wrote on φυσιολογία. It should be remembered that the word is derived from φύειν, "to grow," and that the connotation of spontaneous growth tends accordingly to be present in all early Greek discussions of nature (φύσις).

3. Anaximander's word is τὸ ἄπειρον, variously translated "the boundless," "the non-limited" (K. Freeman), "the infinite" (Burnet), and "the indefinite." My phrase, "boundless reservoir of potential qualities," indicates the fuller significance of the word as I understand it. According to Anaximander, as reported by Diogenes Laertius (II. 1), the Boundless is a basic principle (ἀρχή) and basic element (στοιχεῖον). Diogenes adds the explanation, which he appears to attribute to Anaximander, that the parts undergo change whereas the whole (τὸ πᾶν) does not.

An objection has been raised against the phrase, "boundless reservoir of potential qualities," on the ground that a clear idea of the potential as distinguished from the actual was not formulated until a century and a half later by Aristotle, and that the application of such words to Anaximander's doctrine is anachronistic. The warning should be heeded: any use of later terminologies for an earlier doctrine is likely to be misleading. But the same danger confronts us everywhere, more or less, when we try to express relatively primitive and coalescent ideas by means of a more sophisticated language. At least we can say that the idea of potentiality lay potentially and implicitly in Anaximander's notion of a reservoir of unmanifest qualities.

4. Under the heading "Anaximander" Diels-Kranz lists this as fr. B-1, whereas in Diels it is listed as fr. 9. "Reparation": τίσις. "Justice": δίκη. The word "therein" corresponds to no particular word in the Greek, but indicates the connoted relation.

5. Anaximenes, fr. 2, in Diels-Kranz's "B" list, p. 95. "Soul" represents the word ψυχή and "breath" the word πνεῦμα. In the

present context πνεῦμα evidently carries more of a physical meaning than the other word. Six centuries later, when St. Paul used the word πνεῦμα to mean "spirit," the relation between the two words had become virtually reversed.

6. The four quotations from Xenophanes represent his frs. 15, 23, 24, and 25 in Diels-Kranz's list, pp. 132-135.

7. The question of the relation between Heraclitus and Hippasus of Metapontum is of interest, both generally and because of the attacks which Heraclitus makes against Pythagoras in Frs. 128 and 136 (Appendix C) as well as in the accusation (Diogenes Laertius VIII. 6, rejected by Diels-Kranz as a quotation) that his philosophy is a mere accumulation of secondhand learning. Three questions need to be considered.

A. As to the partial similarity between the doctrines of the two philosophers. Aristotle declares: "Fire is the material principle according to Hippasus and Heraclitus" (*Metaphysics* I: 984 a, 7; cf. *De Caelo* III: 303 b, 12). Diogenes Laertius: "Hippasus of Metapontum was another Pythagorean, who held . . . that the All is limited and ever in motion" (R. D. Hicks' translation in the Loeb Classical Library edition of Diogenes Laertius: II, pp. 397-398).

B. As to the relative dates. Several scholars take Hippasus to be later than Heraclitus. Theodor Gomperz speaks of him as one "who followed in Heraclitus' footsteps" and calls him "an eclectic philosopher . . . who sought to reconcile the teaching of Heraclitus with that of Pythagoras" (*Greek Thinkers*, I, pp. 146, 371). Zeller (p. 195) calls him a later Pythagorean who was influenced by Heraclitus. R. D. Hicks (*loc. cit.*) even places him as late as the fourth century B.C. On the other hand, Proclus describes him as "an early Pythagorean" (*Commentary on Euclid*, Friedländer ed., p. 426, cited in Kirk and Raven, p. 231). And probably Aristotle regarded him as Heraclitus' predecessor, for when mentioning the two men together he places the name of Hippasus first although that of Heraclitus was the better known. Finally, Suidas (Diels-Kranz, p. 143) declares: "Some have said that he [Heraclitus] was a pupil of Xenophanes and of Hippasus the Pythagorean."

C. As to the charge that Hippasus was not a good Pythagorean. The charge is made by Iamblichus in his *Life of Pythagoras*. But since Iamblichus was a devout Pythagorean, while Hippasus was something of an intellectual rebel (cf. Burnet, p. 94, n. 2) who moreover, according to legend, had been shipwrecked for having revealed the Pythagorean mystery of the incommensurability between the hypotenuse and side of a right-angled isosceles triangle, it would seem that the charge against him must be taken with caution. There remain the testimonies that he had at least been a member of the sect. Probably he was not a very orthodox Pythagorean, but he may possibly have provided some sort of loose link between certain teachings of the Pythagorean school and Heraclitus.

8. The two lines of Parmenides' verses to which reference is made are the last two in fr. 6 in Diels-Kranz's "B" list under "Parmenides" (p. 233). "To be and not to be" is expressed by the phrase, τὸ πέλειν τε καὶ οὐκ εἶναι. The final phrase, which might be referring to Fr. 117 of Heraclitus, is: πάντων δὲ παλίντροπός ἐστι κέλευθος.

9. Karl Reinhardt, *Parmenides* (1916), esp. pp. 155ff.

10. The essay is to be found at the beginning of Book IX of his *Lives and Opinions of Eminent Philosophers*, in Vol. II of the Loeb Classical Library edition of Diogenes. Although the gossipy anecdotes that Diogenes likes to tell may have little if any relation to historical truth, there is no reason to doubt his information as to the place, time, and lineage of the philosopher; nor is there reason to doubt the accuracy of his few direct quotations, most of which are represented in the list of accepted Fragments.

11. See Nietzsche, *Gesammelte Werke* (Musarion Verlag edition, Munich, 1920-1928), XIV, p. 75; XV, p. 223; XVI, p. 224; XVII, p. 136; *et passim*. Those who are strong, Nietzsche declares, strive away from one another with as natural a necessity as the weak strive toward one another. Such passion of distance with respect to others, he adds, is the basis on which to promote "that yet more mysterious passion—that craving for more and more extension of distance within one's own soul," which leads toward that ever greater tension which is the "self-overcoming of man."

An attempt to regard Heraclitus as a pessimist in the manner of Schopenhauer was made, for instance, by Gottfried Mayer (see Bibliography).

12. The practice of dedicating a book in a temple was not unusual. Plutarch tells of a poetess who, having won a prize at the Isthmia for her poetry, reverently deposited a scroll of it in the temple at Delphi. Moreover someone, whether the poet himself or another, had dedicated the poems of Hesiod at Mount

Helicon, where Pausanias reports having seen them engraved on ancient tablets of lead. Nor was the dedicatory custom confined to poems. Oenopides of Chios dedicated a bronze copy of an astronomical table at Olympia, Xenocrates dedicated at a shrine on Mount Olympus his calculation of the height of the mountain, Eudoxus dedicated his astronomy at Delos, and a Carthaginian traveler named Hanno dedicated the log book of his travels in the temple of Baal at Carthage. These and other instances are collected by W. H. D. Rouse in *The Votive Offerings* (Cambridge University Press, 1902, p. 64). Cf. Pausanias IX. 31. 4.

13. In the pseudo-Aristotelian treatise, *De Mundo* (v:396 b, 20) Heraclitus is called "the obscure" (ὁ σκοτεινός); Diogenes Laertius quotes a saying that he is "riddling" (αἰνικτής); Tertullian speaks of him with apparent contempt as *ille tenebrosus*; while Clement of Alexandria declares of him that "he loved to conceal his metaphysics in the language of the Mysteries," and the remark has been widely quoted. Aristotle (*Rhetoric* III. v: 1407 b, 13-15) says: "To punctuate Heraclitus is no easy task, because we cannot tell whether a particular word belongs to what precedes or to what follows." Whatever truth there may be in these charges, the main reason for the obscurity and difficulty in Heraclitus was not anything so simple and naïve as a wish to mystify, but rather a need to speak appropriately and not too inadequately of that Nature which surprises us with the unexpected, which does not affirm or deny but merely gives signs, and which loves to hide (Frs. 19, 18, 17 respectively).

14. "Lastly, there are Idols which have immigrated into men's minds from the various dogmas of philosophies, and also from wrong laws of demonstration. These I call *Idols of the Theatre*; because in my judgment all the received systems are but so many stage-plays, representing worlds of their own creation after an unreal and scenic fashion. Nor is it only of the systems now in vogue, or only of the ancient sects and philosophies, that I speak; for many more plays of the same kind may yet be composed and in like artificial manner set forth; seeing that errors the most widely different have nevertheless causes for the most part alike. Neither again do I mean this only of entire systems, but also of many principles and axioms in science, which by tradition, credulity and negligence have come to be received." Francis Bacon, *The Great Instauration* (1620): Part II, "Which is called The New Organon; or, True

Directions Concerning the Interpretation of Nature," Sec. xliv.

Ignoring the particular examples of the Fourth Idol which Bacon later gives by way of illustration, and which represent certain intellectual dangers of his day rather than of ours, we need to be vigilant in all of our thinking lest we fall into an analogous fault. In undertaking to study a distant thinker such as Heraclitus are we in danger of being hindered by "stage-plays, representing worlds of our own creation after an unreal and scenic fashion"? I think we are. To discover our own *Idola Theatri* is much more difficult than to discover those of other persons and of remote civilizations and to label them after our own fashion. Nevertheless a clue to self-discovery in this respect is available for those who wish it. Everett Dean Martin once popularized the adage, "A man is known by the dilemmas he keeps." Each of us has certain preferred ways of setting up alternatives, hence of asking questions, or of setting his own interpretations upon questions that have already been raised. When any favorite pair of alternatives becomes so stereotyped that all our questions (however apparently free and far-ranging they may be) are asked in terms of that particular "either-or," or are asked as covertly presupposing it, that is equivalent to saying that an Idol of the Theater has grown up and taken possession, usually unconscious possession, of our minds. There are two such Idols of the Theater—two strongly held ways of presupposing what the possible types of reply are to a given question—which are current today and which, unless we can look beyond them, will be barriers to an adequate understanding of Heraclitus. They are: (1) the alternatives of subjective vs. objective, or mind vs. matter, or self vs. the world; and (2) the alternatives of a somehow loosely Christian way of thinking about religion vs. a rejection of the possibilities represented by religion altogether. The result is that two of "the dilemmas that we keep" tend to take their shape from these Idols: we ask (1) whether such a thing as goodness, or beauty, or a heard sound, is in me (i.e., purely subjective and relative) *or* in the world itself (in the sense that houses and trees are there); and we ask (2) whether the Christian picture of God and the after-life is true *or* whether all religion is merely fanciful. Now from the point of view represented by these two ways of formulating questions (these two Idols of the Theater) Heraclitus will appear to violate the law of contradiction with respect to the former, since for him the Logos is both subjective and objective at once (as, indeed, is the *tao* of the ancient Chinese, the *dharma* of Hinduism, and the holy *pneuma* of early Christianity), and he will appear to violate the law of excluded middle with respect to the latter, since his notion of divinity (cf. Frs. 61, 62, 63, 64, 74, 104, 105, 106, and 119) and his notion of the after-life (cf. Frs. 59, 65, 67, 68) open up possibilities that are not included in either of our familiar post-Christian alternatives.

15. In his *Conversations with Goethe*, under the date October 29, 1823, Eckermann quotes Goethe as saying: "Every character, however peculiar it may be, and every representation, from stone all the way up the scale to man, has a certain universality; for everything repeats itself, and there is nothing in the world that has happened only once." Fritz Strich, commenting on this and similar passages, remarks: "The symbol is thus, in Goethe's sense, the fullest coalescence of the particular instance and a general idea" (*Der Dichter und die Zeit*, Bern, 1947). Likewise Coleridge praises Shakespeare for effecting a "union and interpenetration of the universal and the particular" (*Lectures on Shakespeare*). A part of the aim of authentic poetry is to unbar the representations of logical language and categorizing thought by rehabilitating certain earlier models of perceiving, thinking, and saying.

16. Aristotle (*De Anima* III. ii) on the relation of perception to what is perceived, and Chap. iv, on the relation of mind to that which is intellectually apprehended.

17. The phrase was used by John Keats in a letter to his brother George, December 1817, apropos of *King Lear*: "It struck me what quality went to form a man of achievement, especially in literature, and which Shakespeare possesses so enormously. I mean *negative capability*; that is, when a man is capable of being in uncertainties, mysteries, doubts, without any irritable reaching after fact and reason."

CHAPTER I. THE WAY OF INQUIRY

1. Sextus (cf. note to Fr. 1 in Appendix B) calls Fr. 1 a "prefatory statement" (προειρημένον) and says that it gives a clue to the scope (περιέχον) of Heraclitus' treatise on nature.

2. Burnet writes: "The λόγος is primarily the discourse of Herakleitos [*sic*] himself; though, as he is a prophet, we may call it his 'Word.'" For the remainder of his argument see Burnet, p. 133, n. 1. Cf. note to Fr. 118 (Appendix B).

3. Wilamowitz in his edition of Euripides' *Herakles* adduces evidence to support his view that the more archaic Greek writers did not employ titles descriptive of the contents of the work, but simply began with the declaration, "So-and-so speaks as follows" (λέγει τάδε). The Pythagorean physician Alcmaeon, roughly contemporary with Heraclitus, opens his treatise with the words: "These are the words of Alcmaeon of Croton, son of Pirithous, which he spoke to Brontinus, Leon, and Bathyllus. . . ." However, since Alcmaeon lived in Italy, his practice offers no strong evidence regarding Heraclitus. At any rate, a number of scholars subscribe to Diels' opinion that Heraclitus' treatise probably began in some such manner.

4. "The common and divine Logos": τὸν κοινὸν λόγον καὶ θεῖον. "By participation in which": οὗ κατὰ μετοχὴν. Sextus Empiricus, *loc. cit.* (in Note 1), Sec. 131. It might be objected that I prejudice the argument by capitalizing "Logos" (λόγος); but it is equally possible that the use of a small initial letter might prejudice the argument in the contrary direction. I employ a capital only when, as here, the context makes it evident that the primary reference is cosmological.

5. The view that what is perceived by many observers is trustworthy—provided they do not have "barbarian souls" (Fr. 13)—and that what is perceived unsharably by a single observer is false, represents an important postulate upon which the structures of physical science have been erected. The scientific method that had been developed at Miletus involved a greater emphasis upon shared observation than was to be found in the visionary wisdom of poets and "wise men" (σοφοί). But in the few extant fragments of the Milesian philosophers there is no evidence that they had endeavored to formulate the nature of the newly objective method that they were beginning to employ. Heraclitus was more explicitly aware of the problem, as Frs. 1, 2, 3, 5, 11, and 15 especially indicate. No doubt the widely shared type of experience that is employed in science needs to be, and inevitably is, supplemented by some degree of private insight as well; and surely no reader of Heraclitus will say that such insight is lacking in his utterances. Nevertheless, it was of great importance in the early development of science to have the claims of objective observation recognized; and Heraclitus contributed signally to such recognition.

6. Epicharmus, fr. 57 (Diels-Kranz, p. 208). In contrasting

the divine λόγος with human calculation Epicharmus employs the word λογισμός for the latter idea.

7. Kirk and Raven, p. 188. Most of what Kirk and Raven write on the subject is excellent, but their use of the word "formula" as applied to the Logos strikes me as gravely misleading.

8. Thus Heraclitus is enabled to say in Fr. 81 that men should speak *with rational awareness* (ξὺν νῷ) and thereby hold on strongly to that which is shared *in common* (τῷ ξυνῷ). Cf. Notes to Frs. 2 and 81 (Appendix B).

CHAPTER II. UNIVERSAL FLUX

1. I follow the custom of translating γένεσις and φθορά by the compounds "coming-to-be" and "passing-away." Simpler pairs of words, such as "creation" and "destruction," or "appearance" and "disappearance," are likely to carry misleading connotations.

2. Aristotle *Physics* I. vi: 189 a, 22ff. Aristotle adds: "The same difficulties hold for every other pair of opposites: Love is not to be thought of [vs. Empedocles' theory] as gathering up Strife and creating something out of it, nor can Strife do this to Love, but rather both of them must operate on a third something." His illustrations are designed to support his contention, against Heraclitus, that an adequate explanation of the world requires more than the principle of duality (opposition, strife), that it requires also the principle of triadicity, in the sense that any adequate conception of change involves three notions—of a prior state, a posterior state, and a "something that remains unchanged throughout the process."

3. "War and Zeus are the same thing": τὸν πόλεμον καὶ τὸν Δία τὸν αὐτὸν εἶναι, καθάπερ καὶ τὸν Ἡράκλειτον λέγειν. Philodemus, in *Dox.*, p. 548, with a few missing letters restored by Diels.

4. On destiny and necessity: Ἡράκλειτος πάντα καθ᾽ εἱμαρμένην, τὴν δὲ αὐτὴν ὑπάρχειν ἀνάγκην. Stobaeus and Plutarch, in *Dox.*, p. 322. Cf. Theophrastus, who says of Heraclitus that "he posits a certain order and a definite time in which cosmic change comes about in accordance with a certain destined necessity" (κατά τινα εἱμαρμένην ἀνάγκην)—*Dox.*, p. 476.

5. Aristotle *Physics* II. iv-vi: 195 b, 31-197 a, 13, on chance; and II. ix: 199 b, 34-200 b, 9 on necessity. Just how Aristotle intends to relate these two concepts is a controversial question; but he seems to me to regard them as alike in that they represent,

in different perspectives, the kind of occurrence or the aspect of occurrence that is independent of intelligent purpose. A chance event can be defined (so I interpret 198 a, 5-7) as an unpurposed and hence "necessary" event which happens to affect some human interest favorably or unfavorably, so that it looks as if it had occurred for the sake of that human interest or in order to thwart it, although in fact it did not.

CHAPTER III. THE PROCESSES OF NATURE

1. Oswald Spengler takes fire as a symbol of πάντα ῥεῖ, which he interprets as the "formal principle" of physical nature (*Der metaphysische Grundgedanke der herakleitischen Philosophie*, A. I. 3). This he calls "the first formulation" (*die erste Formulierung*) of Heraclitus' doctrine, as distinguished from "the second formulation," the principle of paradox.

2. Gustave Teichmüller, *Neue Studien zur Geschichte der Begriffe*, Heft I, p. 2 *et passim*. The tendency to regard Heraclitus as an Ionian philosopher carrying on the tradition of Miletus, and hence to take his concept of fire in a purely physical sense, is an oversimplification that is found in a number of writers (e. g., Julio Navarro Monzó, *La Búsqueda Presocrática*) and has unfortunately become lodged in several textbooks.

3. Aristotle *De Caelo* III. v: 303 b, 12.

4. Aristotle *Metaphysics* I. iii: 984 a, 7.

5. The main Greek commentators on Aristotle quite generally take the Heraclitean concept of fire in a material sense. Asclepius repeatedly refers to Heraclitus' fire in a context which shows that he considers it as playing a role analogous to that of water in Thales' system and of air in the system of Anaximenes, which he describes by the phrase, εἶναι πρῶτον αἴτιον ὑλικόν (*Commentaria in Aristotelem Graeca* VI, Pt. II, p. 25; cf. p. 148, line 19). Elsewhere Asclepius says of Heraclitus and the Milesians jointly that each one of them took one of the physical elements (in Heraclitus' case, fire) to be "a bodily and material principle" (σωματικὴν ἀρχὴν ἐποίουν καὶ ὑλικήν).

Alexander Aphrodisiensis indicates a similar view in his commentary on Aristotle's *Metaphysics*, in *Comm. Ar. Gr.* I, p. 45. Later, however, (*op.cit.*, p. 670) he speaks of the Heraclitean fire as being not only ἀρχή but also οὐσία. The use of the latter word suggests that he may have had something more than a physical principle in mind, but without making clear what it is.

Simplicius, in *Comm. Ar. Gr.* VII, p. 621, says that Heraclitus regarded fire as the "primary bodily principle" (πρῶτον τῶν σωμάτων).

6. "Fire for him [Heraclitus] was neither a mere symbol of the universal process nor a substrate persisting as identical throughout its qualitative alterations. He speaks of it both as a token for exchange like gold in trade and as involved in change itself; and it was the easier for him in this case to identify the sign and the thing signified, since fire does appear to be the one existing phenomenon that is nothing but change."—Harold Cherniss, "The Characteristics and Effects of Presocratic Philosophy," *Journal of the History of Ideas*, xii (1951), p. 331.

7. Hippolytus' words are: λέγει δὲ καὶ φρόνιμον τοῦτο εἶναι τὸ πῦρ καὶ τῆς διοικήσεως τῶν ὅλων αἴτιον. Legge's translation runs: "But he also says that this fire is discerning and the cause of the government of the universe." Thereupon follows the statement which is Fr. 30: "And he calls it craving and satiety."

Stobaeus' words are: Ἡράκλειτος οὐ κατὰ χρόνον εἶναι γενητὸν τὸν κόσμον, ἀλλὰ κατ᾽ ἐπίνοιαν (*Dox.*, p. 331). A translation is given in the text. Kirk (p. 356) suggests that Heraclitus may have considered not all fire to be rational, but only fire of the purest and most ethereal sort.

8. The seventeenth century chemist Robert Boyle speaks of "those two most grand and most catholic principles of bodies, matter and motion" (*Works*, iv, p. 72, "On the Excellence of the Mechanical Principle"). The word "motion" in Boyle's context means movement *in space*, not qualitative change. It is therefore both more exact and semantically more restricted than the Greek word κίνησις. The acceptance of spatial movement as ontologically prior to other kinds of change is so deeply ingrained in our contemporary thinking that we must make a deliberate effort to realize that the Greeks for the most part did not share this presupposition; and certainly Heraclitus did not. Cf., by contrast, W. A. Heidel, "Qualitative Change in Pre-Socratic Philosophy," in *Archiv zur Geschichte der Philosophie*, 19 (1906), pp. 333-379.

9. Aristotle (*De Caelo* iii. v: 304 a, 10ff.). The analogy on which the second argument is based, he says, is this: "The finest body is fire, while among figures the pyramid is primary and has the smallest parts." Simplicius' comment, denying that Heraclitus conceived of fire in terms of pyramids is to be found in *Commentaria in Aristotelem Graeca*, vii, p. 621, lines 7ff.

10. Epicurus' reference to the πρηστήρ is in his letter to Pythocles, Secs. 104-105: Epicurus, *The Extant Remains*, ed.

Cyril Bailey (Oxford, 1926), p. 71. In Lucretius the word πρηστήρ occurs in Book VI, line 424; his meteorological description in lines 423-450 is relevant to the subject. Cyril Bailey's quoted remark occurs in his commentary on line 424, in Vol. III, p. 1618, of his edition of Lucretius (Oxford, 1947). Seneca's reference to the same phenomenon is in his *Quaestiones Naturales* v. xiii. 3. Cf. Burnet, pp. 149-150; Kirk, pp. 325-331.

11. Kirk, p. 356. Plutarch evidently considers the πρηστήρ and the κεραυνός as phenomena of much the same type: *Dox.*, p. 275, line 2.

12. Aëtius-Plutarch, in *Dox.*, p. 276.

13. "We come into existence by an efflux from air": κατ᾽ ἔκποιαν τούτου γιγνόμεθα, where the word τούτου refers to ἀήρ in the preceding clause: Anaximenes, fr. 3 in Diels-Kranz. Although the fragment is repudiated in Diels-Kranz as *"gefälschtes"*—i.e., as probably not the actual words employed by Anaximenes—this possibility does not affect the point made in the chapter.

14. Kirk, p. 115, declares of Fr. 34 that "the presence of air shows that we are dealing with a Stoicized version of Heraclitus." While this *may* be so, my argument in the chapter is intended to show another possibility.

15. Plutarch, *On the E at Delphi*, 392 C.

16. Galenus, *Historia Philosophiae*, in *Dox.*, p. 626.

17. Both passages mentioning the alleged theory of Heraclitus that air is primary are to be found in Sextus Empiricus, *Against the Physicists* (Vol. III of the Loeb Classical Library edition). The former passage is in Bk. I. 360 (*ibid.*, pp. 173, 175); where my phrase "the primary and fundamental elements" is a translation of ἀρχὴ καὶ στοιχεῖον. The latter passage, declaring on the authority of Aenesidemus that Heraclitus held the primary existent (τὸ ὄν) to be air, is in Bk. II, Sec. 233 (*ibid.*, p. 325) of the same essay.

18. Cf. Mircea Eliade, *The Myth of the Eternal Return* (Bollingen Series, XLV; Pantheon Books, 1954), particularly Chapter II, "The Regeneration of Time."

19. Kirk, pp. 336-338. Although Kirk's fifth point seems to comprise two distinct arguments, I have followed his numbering. His pages 307-335, involving interpretations of Frs. 29, 32, and 33 (corresponding to Diels 30 and 31) are indirectly relevant.

20. Plato *Sophist* 242 D-E.

21. See, for instance, the *Theaetetus* 152 E, ff., where the Platonic Socrates is attacking the doctrine, evidently still in-

fluential, that all things that we say "exist" are really in process of becoming—a doctrine that he ascribes loosely to a "whole series of philosophers," including Protagoras, Heraclitus, Empedocles, and even Homer.

22. Aristotle *De Caelo* I. x: 279 b, 15-17. J. L. Stocks' translation (Oxford, 1922) is used here. Stocks interprets Heraclitus as believing "in periodic changes in the constitution of the world as a whole" and that "the world exists, as it were, in a succession of lives." He adds, reasonably I think, that Aristotle's phrase "alternation in the destructive process" is somewhat misleading, since the supposed alternation is rather between generation and destruction—an antithesis which Stock finds analogous to the Love and Strife of Empedocles. Simplicius, in commenting on the passage in *De Caelo*, employs the verbs ἐκπυροῦσθαι and συνίστασθαι to signify respectively the fiery dissolution of the universe in a general conflagration and the subsequent building up of a new universe. (*Commentaria in Aristotelem Graeca* VII, p. 294.)

In an epistle of Plutarch and in Stobaeus' *Eclogues* (compared in parallel columns by Diels, in *Dox.*, pp. 283-284) Heraclitus is quoted as saying: "Fire is the first principle of all things; for all things arise from and eventually pass back into fire." The statement is omitted from the present collection of Fragments, because its authenticity has been challenged by Diels, Bywater, and a majority of classical scholars. Plutarch, whose version is somewhat fuller than that of Stobaeus, goes on to elaborate the intended quotation with the statements that the universe is created through the quenching of the fire, and that after the lengthy process of cosmic creation (what today we call evolution) has been completed, the universe and all the bodies in it (τὸν κόσμον καὶ πάντα τὰ σώματα) are once more (πάλιν δὲ) dissolved by fire in the general conflagration (ἐν τῇ ἐκπυρώσει). Since Plutarch employs indirect discourse in making these statements, he evidently intends them (whether rightly or mistakenly) as quotations from Heraclitus. Granted that some of the language is probably of Stoic origin, there is no reason why the ideas (which are easily envisaged in clear imagery) may not be much older.

23. Aristotle *Physics* III. v: 204b, 35 - 205a, 4. The significant words are: ἀδύνατον τὸ πᾶν . . . ἢ εἶναι ἢ γίγνεσθαι ἕν τι αὐτῶν. ὥσπερ Ἡράκλειτος φησιν ἅπαντα γίγνεσθαί ποτε πῦρ.

On the other hand Cherniss argues that the subject of the

clause referring to Heraclitus is not ἅπαντα but πῦρ. According to this interpretation Heraclitus would be saying not that all things become fire, but that fire becomes all things; hence Aristotle would be citing him (although Cherniss does not say so) as an ally in this instance, instead of as an opponent. That is, he would be drawing upon Heraclitus for confirmation, as though he were to say: "Fire cannot be infinite, existing alone and in the absence of other real things; and indeed Heraclitus agrees, for he says that his fire is constantly becoming other things than itself." See Harold Cherniss, *Aristotle's Criticism of Presocratic Philosophy*, p. 29, n. 108. But it would be a surprising departure from Aristotle's usual attitude if he were to call on Heraclitus for confirmation!

Taking, then, ἅπαντα to be the subject and πῦρ to be the object of the infinitive verb γίγνεσθαι (as most interpreters other than Cherniss have done), the one technical question that remains is whether ἅπαντα is to be understood dissociatively or collectively. That is, does the clause assert that all things are constantly in process of becoming fire (which is the likeliest meaning of Fr. 28) or that at certain times (ποτε) everything becomes fire simultaneously? Zeller is of the opinion that ἅπαντα connotes the simultaneous totality of all things, as distinguished from πάντα which would connote all things discursively and individually. Burnet, on the contrary, denies that there is any appreciable connotative difference between the two expressions. It appears that the debated question cannot be answered by appealing to this word alone.

24. The statement in Aëtius is followed by an explanation, which may be intended as a paraphrase of Heraclitus' views; it is impossible to be sure. The passage runs as follows: "Through the quenching of this fire all the things in the universe are made. First, what is coarsest is drawn off into itself, producing earth; then the earth, through the loosening action of fire, turns into water; the water is evaporated into air; and then once more the universe and all the bodies in it are dissolved by fire in the general conflagration again" (*Dox.*, p. 284).

25. The Pseudo-Aristotelian *De Mundo* 401 a, 8ff.: "All animals, both wild and tame, feeding in the air or on the earth or in the water, are born and mature and decay in obedience to the ordinance of God; for in the words of Heraclitus . . ."—whereupon the Fragment is quoted.

CHAPTER IV. HUMAN SOUL

1. Arius Didymus, in *Dox.*, p. 471, line 2.

2. Aristotle *De Anima* I. i: 403 a, 24: the affections (τὰ πάθη, where "of soul" or "of the soul" is understood) are meanings implicit in matter (λόγοι ἔνυλοι). Later, in Bk. II of *De Anima*, Aristotle defines soul itself as "the first grade of actuality of a natural being having life potentially in it" (412 a, 20-21: J. A. Smith's translation in the Oxford University Press series) and as "the first grade of actuality of a natural organized body" (412 b, 5-6: the same).

3. Theophrastus, in *De Vertigine*, mentions eyesight in particular, for if the motions of the head should stop, or be deranged, the clarity of the visual image would fail. The nature of the image, he observes, is preserved and exists (σώζεται καὶ συμμένει) through this very motion (κίνησις). See Walzer, p. 154.

4. Kirk writes: "Souls use smell in Hades because they are surrounded by dry matter, than which they are but little less dry. When one recalls that the soul in life was by implication characterized as a form of fire, it is not difficult to deduce that Heraclitus' 'Hades' is a realm of fire, in which the disembodied souls are themselves fiery." (G. S. Kirk, in *American Journal of Philology*, 70 [1947], p. 389.) Cf. Appendix B, the Note to Fr. 86.

CHAPTER V. IN RELIGIOUS PERSPECTIVE

1. Euripides, *The Trojan Women*, line 885. Sextus Empiricus quotes the passage as preliminary to a discussion of the Heraclitean Logos.

2. Sextus Empiricus *Against the Logicians* I. 129-130. "The divine Logos" is ὁ θεῖος λόγος. "Intelligent": νοετός. "Mindful again": πάλιν ἔμφρονες.

3. Xenophanes, fr. 15 in Diels-Kranz.

4. Aristotle's mention of Thales' remark that soul is diffused through the entire universe is in *De Anima* I. 5: 411 a, 7-8. Simplicius' commentary is in *Commentaria in Aristotelem Graeca*, XI, p. 73. Thales' statement about the magnet having soul is mentioned by Aristotle in *De Anima* 405 a, 19.

5. Cebes' argument, that the relation of soul to body may be analogous to the relation of body to its clothes—the soul outliving a number of bodies, as the body outlasts a number of pieces of clothing, although neither of them lasts eternally for all that

—is given in Plato's *Phaedo* 87A - 88C. Socrates' reply, such as it is, appears in 95 A-E.

6. My discussion of plurisignation is in *The Burning Fountain* (Indiana University Press, 1954), pp. 61-62, 112-117, 149-151, and, with reference to ancient Greek thinking, pp. 254-255.

7. G. S. Kirk, "Heraclitus and Death in Battle," in *American Journal of Philology*, 70 (1949), p. 390. Cf. Appendix B, the Note to Fr. 86.

CHAPTER VI. MAN AMONG MEN

1. See Note 6 to Chapter VIII. I am not, of course, attributing to Aristotle the extended significance of ἁμαρτία suggested in the text. It may be, as S. H. Butcher says (*Aristotle's Theory of Poetry and Fine Arts*, p. 295) that Aristotle used the word in much the same sense as he normally used ἁμάρτημα, which he defines (*Nicomachean Ethics* v. viii:1135 b 16) as a mistake that could have been avoided. Butcher adds, however, that both words are also occasionally used by Aristotle in the broader sense of error due to unavoidable ignorance, as virtually synonymous with ἀτύχημα, "misfortune." Now, although in the *Ethics* Aristotle maintains a careful distinction between actions done with the power of knowing and actions done in unavoidable ignorance, he says in the *Poetics* (XIV:1453 b 27-31) that the central action of a tragic plot can be of either type, and he mentions the *Oedipus Tyrannus* of Sophocles as an example of the latter. Obviously, of course, Oedipus acted in ignorance of what he was doing; yet Sophocles calls him, in the title, τύραννος, which carries the connotation of *usurper*. Oedipus, then, has usurped; and much of the power of Sophocles' play comes from the implicit sense that a potentially universal human condition is represented by the tragic action. All men are usurpers in some sense; all things, by their very existence, usurp; and such usurpation is, in the broadest sense, a kind of hybris.

2. Cf. Geoffrey S. Kirk, "Heraclitus and Death in Battle," where possible meanings of Fr. 86 are discussed.

3. On the semantic role of the serious pun, see William Empson, *Seven Types of Ambiguity* (Oxford University Press, 1930); and cf. the references in Chapter V, Note 6.

4. Kirk, pp. 50-51. As against Reinhardt, *Parmenides*, pp. 215ff., and Gigon, *Untersuchungen zu Heraklit*, p. 14. The point is not that there was no difference to the ancient mind between

codified laws and unwritten laws—for of course there was, and such unwritten laws as those bearing on one's duties to the gods, to one's parents, and to guests were regarded as the more fundamental—but that *both* these types of law were οἱ ἀνθρώπειοι νόμοι, and as such were secondary to and nourished by the one divine law: ὑπὸ ἑνὸς τοῦ θείου.

5. The episode of Byrsa and the bull's hide is told in the *Aeneid* I. 365-370. The episode of the wooden horse is told in II 234ff. Line 234 itself is of special importance: *Dividimus muros et moenia pandimus urbis.* In order to make the gate large enough for the wooden horse to be dragged through it, the Trojans had to chop asunder a part of their city wall and thereby "open the defenses of the city." Apart from the unknown threat inside the horse, this weakening of the city wall was bad enough from a military point of view, with the enemy lurking a little way off. It was even worse, to the ancient mind, in its symbolical and magical aspect.

CHAPTER VII. RELATIVITY AND PARADOX

1. Asclepius, commentary on Aristotle's *Metaphysics*, in *Commentaria in Aristotelem Graeca*, VI, Pt. II, p. 258.

2. I have developed the distinction between depth language and steno-language in *The Burning Fountain*, pp. 24-29; 48-51.

3. Hippolytus *The Refutation of All Heresies* IX. He describes the motion of the screw by saying, "For the upward way is encompassed by [or cleaves to ?] a circle [or circular motion]" : ἄνω γὰρ ὁμοῦ καὶ κύκλῳ περιέχεται.

4. Alcmaeon of Crotona, Fragment 2 in Diels-Kranz. He is believed to have lived about a generation after Heraclitus. Little else is known about him, and there are only four other surviving fragments of his writing.

CHAPTER VIII. THE HIDDEN HARMONY

1. Hastings' *Encyclopaedia of Religion and Ethics*. After the words, "truth and illusion," Diels inserts the corresponding Greek words that he has in mind, ἀλήθεια and δόξα.

2. Hermann Fränkel, "Heraclitus on God and the Phenomenal World": *American Philological Association, Proceedings,* 69 (1938), pp. 230ff.

3. *Phaedo* 85 E, ff. Simmias, a Pythagorean, uses the word

ἁρμονία as connoting "right proportion among such bodily elements as hot and cold, moist and dry." If this were all, Kirk's nonmusical interpretation of the word might appear to be justified. But in the previous sentence Simmias has been speaking of the ἁρμονία produced by the strings of a lyre; from which the nature of his metaphoric image is evident.

4. Aristotle (*Nicomachean Ethics* VIII. i:1155 b, 5) ostensibly quotes Heraclitus as saying that the fairest ἁρμονία is produced from opposing tones (ἐκ τῶν διαφερόντων, where the word for "tones" is evidently to be understood). Aristotle connects this with the statements, which he also attributes to Heraclitus, that opposites unite and that all things occur through strife. Diels-Kranz does not accept these remarks as authentic Heraclitean quotations, however.

5. Edmund Pfleiderer, *Die Philosophie des Heraklit von Ephesus im Lichte der Mysterienidee*, p. 89.

6. Aristotle *Poetics* XIII:1453 a, 10, where effective tragedy is said to occur δὶ ἁμαρτίαν τινά. The cognate verb ἁμαρτάνειν can be seen developing its metaphorical meaning in Homer; for in the *Iliad* (v. 287) it is applied to a spear's missing its mark, and by the time of the *Odyssey* (XXI. 155) it has come to mean, "to fail of one's purpose."

7. Marcus Aurelius *Meditations* VI. 42. The passage in which the quotation occurs runs as follows, in Long's translation: "We are all working together to one end, some with knowledge and design, and others without knowing what they do; as men also when they are asleep, of whom it was Heraclitus, I think, who says that they are laborers and coöperators in the things that take place in the universe. But men coöperate after different fashions; and even those coöperate abundantly who find fault with what happens and those who try to oppose it and to hinder it; for the universe has need even of such men as these."

APPENDIX B

NOTES ON THE FRAGMENTS

Since the philosophy of Heraclitus is available to us only through quotations of him and references to him made by later ancient writers, an editor attempting to reconstruct the original doctrine faces two kinds of problem. The one, the problem of interpretation, arises in connection with any philosophy that may be studied, although the problem is likely to be more acute when the philosophy survives only in a fragmentary state. The other problem, which arises when a philosopher's utterances are known only through quotations by others, has to do with authenticity. My own judgments of authenticity are represented by the one hundred and twenty-four Fragments contained in the present list—not counting the authentic but nugatory bits that I have relegated to Appendix C. Although in the main my judgments of authenticity have been guided by those of Diels (fifth edition, as revised by Kranz, 1934), it will be found that I have included five Fragments (20, 27, 43, 62, 74) that were omitted from the Diels-Kranz list. My reasons for accepting them are stated in each case.

One's interpretation of a particular Fragment, as of a word within a Fragment, often requires (besides a dictionary knowledge of the meaning of the words employed) two kinds of critical examination, which must sometimes be balanced against each other. The meaning of a quotation, wherever it is in doubt, must be studied in relation both to the doxographical context and to whatever other relevant evidences there are concerning Heraclitus' views on the subject involved. On the one hand we must try to be critically aware of how and why a certain writer introduces a quotation from Heraclitus, and must consider whether the writer's general attitude and purpose might be such as to tempt him to give the quotation an emphasis or a twist that may be foreign to the original intention. On the other hand, we sometimes have to raise the question, "Does this or that interpretation of word or sentence fit in with what we judge, from other Heraclitean quotations and to some extent from peripheral evidence, that Heraclitus most probably would have meant?" This sort of criterion is an especially risky one when applied to a philosophy so full of paradoxes as that of Heraclitus; nevertheless it cannot be altogether avoided.

Suppose, for example, we are considering Clement of Alexandria's quotation of Fr. 19, which is here translated, "Unless you expect the unexpected you will never find [truth]; for it is hard to discover and hard to attain." A lively dispute has raged over the question of whether there should or should not be a grammatical break after the third word, ἔλπηται. If the traditional reading is accepted, as given by Diels, retaining the comma after the third word, then the translations of Fairbanks (republished in Nahm's well-known volume of pre-Socratic philosophers) and of Kathleen Freeman are appropriate: "If one does not hope, one will not find the un-hoped for" (Freeman). If, on the other hand, Gomperz's suggested emendation of the traditional reading is accepted and the grammatical break is delayed until after the fourth word, ἀνέλπιστον, then the latter word becomes the object of the foregoing verb, and the meaning becomes, as expressed by Burnet: "If you do not expect the unexpected, you will not find it; for it is hard to be sought out and difficult." (The antecedent of "it" has been lost; I assume that it expressed in some manner the general but elusive object of one's highest search.) Now unquestionably the Diels punctuation, and not the Gomperz emendation, is in line with the way in which Clement himself understood and reported the passage, as shown both by the manuscript reading and by Clement's context. But since probably no sign for the comma-break had been in use when Heraclitus wrote, and since conventions of comma-usage were still fitful in Clement's day, it is easy to see why Clement might in good faith have shifted the position of the break from where Heraclitus had intended it should be. In such a situation our examination of the doxographical context can bring to light some of the ideas that might have been present in Clement's mind to produce such an unconscious alteration of the original meaning. Now if Clement's misinterpretation is to be taken not as an abstract possibility but as a significant hypothesis, then we must look back also to whatever we can soundly infer regarding the original context—I mean, of course, not the original verbal context, of which we know nothing, but the original philosophical context, consisting of Heraclitus' characteristic ways of thinking and expressing himself— in order to have a basis for judging how the passage was most probably meant when it was first written.

In the case of the present Fragment, an examination of the doxographical context shows that Clement's purpose in introducing the quotation was to let it stand parallel to his immediately preceding quotation from Isaiah, vii. 9, which in the Revised Standard Version reads: "If you will not believe, surely you shall not be established." The word that is translated "believe" in the modern Bibles appeared as the verb πιστεύειν in the Greek text that Clement was using; his quotation runs, ἐὰν μὴ πιστεύσητε, οὐδὲ μὴ συνῆτε. Thus it seems evident that Clement was taking the verbs πιστεύειν and ἐλπίζειν as respectively connoting the ideas of faith and hope, which St. Paul had memorably united in the texture of Christian thought. On recognizing this contextual tie-up in Clement's *Stromata* our minds naturally pass, as the next critical step, to the question: "But would Heraclitus' own doctrine have contained any such connection of ideas?" Obviously the only possible answer here is "No"; for while we cannot be sure of what Heraclitus' original context of the remark may have been, we can be sure of some of the things it was not, and the Clementine Christian association of ideas is one of them. As a matter of fact, I believe we can go even a step further, and affirm that the paradox "expect the unexpected" appears, from what else we know of the Ephesian's style, to be rather distinctively and happily Heraclitean in tone, in a way that Clement's version is not. Accordingly it seems to me we have sufficiently objective grounds for rejecting the translations published by Fairbanks (1898), Nahm (1935, employing the Fairbanks translation), and Kathleen Freeman (1948), and for accepting those of Burnet (given above) and R. Walzer (*"Se alcuno mai non speri l'inspearabile, non lo troverà"*).

A different sort of problem arises in the case of another Christian doxographer, Hippolytus. Like Clement he shows a marked Christian bias, but his bias does not appear to diminish his reliability when he is quoting from pagan sources, particularly from Heraclitus. This is the almost universal opinion of modern scholars; it is supported both by scattered evidence from comparison with other versions of a quoted Fragment offered by other writers, and also deductively from the nature and circumstances of his writing. The former kind of evidence can be discovered by comparing Fr. 66, taken from Hippolytus, with the variant form given by Clement; for as I argue in my note to the Fragment in the present Appendix, it is psychologically more plausible to regard Hippolytus' as the original and Clement's as the variant version rather than the other way round.

To this type of specific evidence, which can be adduced in the case of several of the Fragments, there can be added a general consideration, drawn from the character of Hippolytus' thinking and composition. His purpose in writing *The Refutation of All Heresies* he frankly avows. It is to demonstrate that the major Christian heresies up to his time had been produced not by a corruption of Christian faith from within, but by an infiltration of pagan ideas and beliefs. In the ninth book he deals with the heresy of Noetus, who had violated the orthodox creed by overstressing the identity of Father and Son; and he undertakes to show that Noetus and his followers, "who delude themselves into thinking they are disciples of Christ," are actually influenced by the teachings of Heraclitus and Stoicism. In carrying out this pious aim Hippolytus shows a strangely defective sense of logical connections. Choosing some of the most paradoxical of Heraclitus' utterances (a choice for which we may well be grateful) he throws them together in a hit-or-miss fashion, occasionally making farfetched comparisons with elements of Christian doctrine. For instance, he introduces Fr. 68, "They will arise into wakefulness and become guardians of the living and the dead," by explaining that Heraclitus is here affirming "that there is a resurrection of this palpable flesh in which we are born." Fr. 25 ("War is both father and king of all . . .") and the latter half of Fr. 24 ("The royal power is a child's") he takes as distorted and proto-heretical references to, respectively, Father and Son in the Christian Trinity. Surely anyone enjoying so loose a sense of interpretative relevance as these passages evince would scarcely have reason for wishing to misquote; for any quotations of a strikingly paradoxical character would serve his turn, and there must have been plenty of such material to be found in Heraclitus' treatise as it stood. It is Hippolytus' very lack of relational clarity that makes his individual quotations the more reliable.

Among the non-Christian writers, too, a critical reserve must guard our acceptance of alleged quotations. In the case of Plato and Aristotle, as I have argued elsewhere, there is reason to suspect that at times their references to Heraclitus are colored and perhaps exacerbated by the somewhat too provocative opinions of contemporary neo-Heracliteans. In the case of Diogenes Laertius the fault is likely to be a gossipy irresponsibility, and a scholar has the responsibility of judging which of his remarks are likely to have been affected by it and which not. In the cases of Plutarch and Sextus Empiricus it is not always easy to discover the line between the quoted saying of Heraclitus and philosophical supplementations that come either from Stoic sources or from these writers themselves. Recognizing such tendentious characteristics of the various writers who quote Heraclitus is a necessary part of critical procedure.

My readings of the Greek text of the Fragments have been guided mainly by Diels-Kranz and Walzer, supplemented wherever possible by the best available edition or editions of the doxographical sources: see Bibliography, Section I. Each Fragment is identified in the present Appendix by the number that introduced it in Chapters I to VIII. In parentheses are given the numbers employed by Diels in his "B" list (adopted by Diels-Kranz, Walzer, Freeman, and virtually all German scholars of the present century) and by Bywater (adopted by Burnet, Fairbanks, and the Loeb Classical Library). Words and phrases that the present editor judges to have had their source not in Heraclitus but in the doxographers who quote him are enclosed in square brackets.

A list of the more important doxographical sources of the Fragments is to be found on page 156.

CHAPTER I. THE WAY OF INQUIRY

Fr. 1 (D 1; By 2). τοῦ δὲ λόγου τοῦδ' ἐόντος ἀεὶ ἀξύνετοι γίνονται ἄνθρωποι καὶ πρόσθεν ἢ ἀκοῦσαι καὶ ἀκούσαντες τὸ πρῶτον· γινομένων γὰρ πάντων κατὰ τὸν λόγον τόνδε ἀπείροισιν ἐοίκασι, πειρώμενοι καὶ ἐπέων καὶ ἔργων τοιούτων. ὁκοίων ἐγὼ διηγεῦμαι κατὰ φύσιν διαιρέων ἕκαστον καὶ φράζων ὅκως ἔχει· τοὺς δὲ ἄλλους ἀνθρώπους λανθάνει ὁκόσα ἐγερθέντες ποιοῦσιν, ὅκωσπερ ὁκόσα εὕδοντες ἐπιλανθάνονται.

The passage is preserved by Sextus Empiricus, in *Adversus Mathematicos* ("Against the Savants"), Bk. VII, Sec. 132. In the Loeb Classical Library edition of Sextus Empiricus, Bk. VII of this treatise is published as Bk. I of "Against the Logicians," but the section numbers correspond. Sextus says that Heraclitus wrote these words "at the outset of his writings on nature" (ἐναρχόμενος οὖν τῶν περὶ φύσεως). Portions of the passage, but not the whole of it, are quoted by Aristotle (*Rhetoric* III. 5), Clement of Alexandria (*Stromata* II, p. 401, in Stählin's edition), and Hippolytus (*Refutation of All Heresies* IX). There have been some disagreements as to how the opening words should be divided into phrases. I follow the practice of Diels (as distinct from Diels-Kranz) and Burnet in taking ἀεὶ as attached to the words standing ahead of it. Kirk, who takes it as going with the words that follow, translates: "Of the Logos which is as I describe it men always prove to be uncomprehending . . ." (Kirk, p. 33; Kirk and Raven, p. 187n.).

In order not to prejudge the meaning of the controversial word λόγος I follow Kirk in not translating it but simply transliterating it as "Logos." Diels translates it *"Wort (Weltgesetz)"*; Diels-Kranz, *"der Lehre Sinn."* The question of the word's meaning is discussed in Chapter 1.

Fr. 2 (D 2; By 92). διὸ δεῖ ἕπεσθαι τῷ ξυνῷ [τουτέστι τῷ κοινῷ· ξυνὸς γὰρ ὁ κοινός]. τοῦ λόγου δ' ἐόντος ξυνοῦ ζώουσιν οἱ πολλοὶ ὡς ἰδίαν ἔχοντες φρόνησιν. Sextus Empiricus, *op.cit.*, Sec. 133. I follow Schleiermacher and Burnet in their reconstruction of the first sentence. This, and not the manuscript reading, makes logical connection with the remainder of the quotation. Bekker's theory is plausible: that the original quotation contained the Heraclitean word τῷ ξυνῷ, that Sextus explained it to his readers by adding the phrase τουτέστι τῷ κοινῷ, and that the words τῷ ξυνῷ τουτέστι were dropped out in copying. The next words, ξυνὸς γὰρ ὁ κοινός, are almost certainly Sextus' gloss, as most scholars agree. Diels-Kranz prints these two sets of words after ξυνῷ as belonging to Sextus rather than to Heraclitus. Walzer, although he includes all the words in his text of the Fragment, limits his translation to the simple statement, "Bisogna perciò seguire il commune." The word φρόνησις, which I translate "intelligence," is translated *"Einsicht"* by Diels and *"saggezza"* by Walzer. In the variant version given by Stobaeus and represented by our Fr. 80 it is intelligence (τὸ φρονεῖν) that is described as common to all.

Fr. 3 (D. 35; By 49). χρὴ [γὰρ] εὖ μάλα πολλῶν ἵστορας φιλοσόφους ἄνδρας εἶναι.

Clement of Alexandria *Stromata* II. 421 (Stählin). Cf. Dindorf's ed., III, p. 119. This is one of the earliest known uses of φιλόσοφος, which is believed to have been of Pythagorean origin.

Fr. 4 (D 22; By 8). χρυσὸν [γὰρ] οἱ διζήμενοι γῆν πολλὴν ὀρύσσουσι καὶ εὑρίσκουσιν ὀλίγον.

Clement *Stromata* II. 249.

Fr. 5 (D 47; By 48). μὴ εἰκῆ περὶ τῶν μεγίστων συμβαλλώμεθα.

Diogenes Laertius IX. 72. Quoted by Diogenes not in his essay on Heraclitus, but in the one on Pyrrho.

Fr. 6 (D 40; By 16). πολυμαθίη νόον ἔχειν οὐ διδάσκει.

Diogenes Laertius ix. 1 (here, as elsewhere unless otherwise stated, a quotation from Diogenes is from his essay on Heraclitus) and Clement, *Stromata* ii. 59. Aulus Gellius, *Noctes Atticae*, Praefatio, 12, makes nearly the same quotation in Latin. Diogenes alone adds the phrase, accepted by Diels-Kranz, "otherwise it would have taught understanding to Hesiod and Pythagoras, to Xenophanes and Hecataeus."

Fr. 7 (D 108; By 18). ὁκόσων λόγους ἤκουσα, οὐδεὶς ἀφικνεῖται ἐς τοῦτο, ὥστε γινώσκειν ὅτι σοφόν ἐστι πάντων κεχωρισμένον.

Stobaeus *Florilegium* iii. 1. Here λόγος in the plural evidently means "discourses."

Fr. 8 (D 101; By 80). ἐδιζησάμην ἐμεωυτόν.

Plutarch *Against Colotes* 1118 C.

Fr. 9 (D 116; By 106). ἀνθρώποισι πᾶσι μέτεστι γινώσκειν ἑωυτοὺς καὶ σωφρονεῖν.

Stobaeus *Florilegium* iii. 5. Diels alters the final word of the manuscript reading to φρονεῖν, and translates "klug zu sein." Diels-Kranz, followed by Walzer, restores the manuscript reading, as here. But Walzer, without stating why, questions the genuineness of the Fragment.

Fr. 10 (D 112; By 107). σωφρονεῖν ἀρετὴ μεγίστη, καὶ σοφίη ἀληθέα λέγειν καὶ ποιεῖν κατὰ φύσιν ἐπαΐοντας.

Stobaeus *Florilegium* iii. 5. Here again, although the manuscripts read σωφρονεῖν, Diels substitutes φρονεῖν, while Diels-Kranz restores the manuscript reading. In this instance the difference of interpretation is not so great, since Diels translates "das Denken" and Diels-Kranz "gesunde Denken." Walzer sides with Diels. In the case of both Frs. 9 and 10 I am unable to see sufficient ground for Diels' alteration of the manuscripts. Fairbanks believes that the two Fragments are not genuine.

Fr. 11 (D 55; By 13). ὅσων ὄψις ἀκοὴ μάθησις, ταῦτα ἐγὼ προτιμέω.

Hippolytus *Refutation of All Heresies* ix. Cf. Snell, in *Hermes*, 61 (1926), p. 362.

Fr. 12 (D 101 a; By 15). ὀφθαλμοὶ [γὰρ] τῶν ὤτων ἀκριβέστεροι μάρτυρες.

Polybius xii. 27.

Fr. 13 (D 107; By 4). κακοὶ μάρτυρες ἀνθρώποισιν ὀφθαλμοὶ καὶ ὦτα βαρβάρους ψυχὰς ἐχόντων.

Sextus Empiricus, *Adversus Mathematicos* vii ("Against the

Logicians," Bk. 1), Sec. 126. Schleiermacher (fr. 22) translates the last three words as "mit rohen Seelen."

Fr. 14 (D 73; By 94). οὐ δεῖ ὥσπερ καθεύδοντας ποιεῖν καὶ λέγειν. Marcus Aurelius IV. 46, where it follows the quotation of Fr. 64.

Fr. 15 (D 89; By 95). τοῖς ἐγρηγορόσιν ἕνα καὶ κοινὸν κόσμον εἶναι, τῶν δὲ κοιμωμένων ἕκαστον εἰς ἴδιον ἀποστρέφεσθαι. Plutarch *On Superstition* 166 C.

Fr. 16 (D 21; By 64). θάνατός ἐστιν ὁκόσα ἐγερθέντες ὁρέομεν, ὁκόσα δὲ εὕδοντες ὕπνος.

Clement *Stromata* II. 205. More literal translations are those of Freeman ("All that we see while slumbering is sleep"), Diels ("Tod ist alles, was wir im Wachen sehen, und Schlaf, was im Schlummer"), and Walzer ("Tutto ciò che vediamo dormienti è sonno"). But in taking care to reproduce the form of the Greek tautology these writers have lost the connotative force of ὕπνος. Not only sleep is meant, but also the kind of awareness that may take place in sleep—i.e., dream. Thus in Plato (*Laws* VII. 800 A) we read: "if one of them had divined it vaguely καθ᾽ ὕπνον"— which could be translated "in sleep," but equally well "in a dream."

Fr. 17 (D 123; By 10). φύσις κρύπτεσθαι φιλεῖ. Found in Themistius, Proclus, and twice in Philo.

Fr. 18 (D 93; By 11). ὁ ἄναξ οὗ τὸ μαντεῖόν ἐστι τὸ ἐν Δελφοῖς οὔτε λέγει οὔτε κρύπτει ἀλλὰ σημαίνει. Plutarch *On the Pythian Oracles* 404 E. Iamblichus *De Mysteriis* III. 15, confirms the quotation, putting it in indirect discourse and using participles in place of verbs. The word σημαίνει, which I have translated "gives signs," appears to have been derived from σῆμα, which had meant "a sign." In early Greek medical vocabulary the σῆμα was a symptom, and σημαίνειν carried the idea of a symptom indicating or suggesting something more than itself. Later, as in Plato's *Phaedo*, the word σῆμα meant "tomb." This meaning appears to have developed out of the practice of placing a mark on the grave to indicate to the god who was buried there. The overtone of religious mystery may still have been present in Heraclitus' use of σημαίνειν, although the direction of communication is now from god to man, not from man to god.

Fr. 19 (D 18; By 7). ἐὰν μὴ ἔλπηται ἀνέλπιστον οὐκ ἐξευρήσει, ἀνεξερεύνητον ἐὸν καὶ ἄπορον. Clement *Stromata* II. 121. ἐὰν μὴ ἔλπηται ἀνέλπιστον οὐκ ἐξευρήσει . . . Fairbanks and Kathleen Freeman are wrong, I think, in taking this to mean, "If one does not hope, one will not find the unhoped for" (Freeman's translation). It does not sound like Heraclitus, and it is not a necessary translation. For ἔλπηται need not mean "hope"; it can also mean "expect," and even "expect anxiously" (Liddell and Scott). Heraclitus probably meant to steer his meaning between the extremes of hope and anxiety. The word ἀνέλπιστον could be the object of either of the two verbs, or perhaps could belong rather loosely to both at once; I am taking it as primarily the object of ἔλπηται and this leaves the object of ἐξευρήσει somewhat vague. I have supplied the word "truth" in order to complete the English sentence; if taken loosely it cannot be too far from Heraclitus' meaning.

CHAPTER II. UNIVERSAL FLUX

Fr. 20 (D—; By—). πάντα ῥεῖ, οὐδὲν δὲ μένει· πάντα χωρεῖ, καὶ οὐδὲν μένει.

The text as here reconstructed is drawn from several well-known passages, varying in expression but alike in purport. The second clause appears in the *Cratylus*, where Plato attributes it to Heraclitus with the words λέγει ὅτι. In the same Dialogue, 440 C, he attributes to the followers of Heraclitus (οἱ περὶ Ἡράκλειτον) the phrase "Everything flows" (πάντα ῥεῖ), separating the two words by what is obviously his own disparaging comment, "like leaky pots." In the *Theaetetus*, 182 C, the word ῥεῖ is coupled with κινεῖται to describe the Heraclitean doctrine, although Heraclitus is not mentioned here. Elsewhere in the *Theaetetus* (182 C-D and 160 D) Plato uses various cognate forms of the verb ῥεῖν to describe the Heraclitean doctrine; at 160 D he curiously ascribes the doctrine to both Heraclitus and Homer. Again, Aristotle in the *Metaphysics* (XIII:1078 b, 14-15) speaks of the doctrine that "all perceptible things flow" (ὡς πάντων τῶν αἰσθητῶν ἀεὶ ῥεόντων) and labels the doctrine "Heraclitean." Although such cumulative evidence may fall short of establishing the words as a direct quotation from Heraclitus, there is hardly any phrase that has been more widely associated with his doctrine in classical times and by later doxographers; and it is indisputably Heraclitean in tone and substance.

Fr. 21 (D 91, 12; By 41). ποταμῷ [γὰρ] οὐκ ἔστιν ἐμβῆναι δὶς τῷ αὐτῷ· ἕτερα καὶ ἕτερα ὕδατα ἐπιρρεῖ.

Plutarch, *On the E at Delphi*, 392 C. Variant versions are

given by Aristotle in the *Metaphysics* (IV: 1010a, 13), by Plutarch in his *Quaestiones Naturales* (912 A), and by Arius Didymus (*Dox.*, p. 471). The last author joins the Fragment somewhat oddly with Fr. 44. Aristotle mentions the remark as if it were already well known as coming from Heraclitus. Diels uses Arius Didymus' version (from which the last five words are taken) as his fr. 12, Plutarch's as his fr. 91.

Fr. 22 (D 126; By 39). τὰ ψυχρὰ θέρεται, θερμὸν ψύχεται, ὑγρὸν αὐαίνεται, καρφαλέον νοτίζεται.

The Fragment is quoted by a scribe named Tzetzes in a commentary on the *Iliad*. I have not been able to verify it there, but the accuracy of the quotation is attested by Bywater, Diels-Kranz, Walzer, and others.

Fr. 23 (D 84a; By 83). μεταβάλλον ἀναπαύεται.

Plotinus *Enneads* IV. viii. 1. The Greek phrase might have either of two meanings. It might be a paradoxical way of saying that everything changes continually; or it might mean (cf. Fr. 89) that there is comfort to be had in changing one's situation. My translation is guided by the former idea, and this is evidently justified by the preceding words in Plotinus: "Heraclitus . . . tells of compulsory alternation from contrary to contrary, speaks of ascent and descent, says that . . ."—and then comes the Fragment. On the other hand the Stephen McKenna translation of Plotinus, as revised by B. S. Page (London, 1953) renders the quotation, "Change reposes"; which evidently implies the second interpretation.

Fr. 24 (D 52; By 79). αἰὼν παῖς ἐστι παίζων, πεσσεύων· παιδὸς ἡ βασιληίη.

Hippolytus IX. The idea of the παῖς παίζων, in varying forms, is attributed to Heraclitus by Clement, Proclus, and Lucian. Plutarch, without mentioning Heraclitus, speaks of "the poet's fancied child playing a game amid the sand that is heaped together and then scattered again by him" (*On the E at Delphi* 393 E; F. C. Babbitt's translation in the Loeb Classical Library edition).

The meaning of αἰών is in question. In Christian Greek vocabulary at the time of Hippolytus the word had come to mean "eternity." Some have held that in Heraclitus' usage it means "the great age"—i.e., the vast stretch of time between two world conflagrations; but others, and particularly those who assign a later Stoic origin to the theory of world conflagrations, reject so definite an interpretation. It seems best to follow the practice of Diels and Burnet in adopting the neutral translation, "time."

Diels-Kranz has altered Diels' *"Zeit"* to *"Lebenszeit,"* and Fairbanks similarly writes "lifetime."

Fr. 25 (D 53; By 44). πόλεμος πάντων μὲν πατήρ ἐστι, πάντων δὲ βασιλεύς, καὶ τοὺς μὲν θεοὺς ἔδειξε τοὺς δὲ ἀνθρώπους, τοὺς μὲν δούλους ἐποίησε τοὺς δὲ ἐλευθέρους.

Hippolytus ix. In this and the following two passages the word "war" is used for πόλεμος and "strife" for ἔρις. Kirk is evidently right in saying (p. 242) that the two words represent the same concept.

Fr. 26 (D 80; By 62). εἰδέναι δὲ χρὴ τὸν πόλεμον ἐόντα ξυνόν, καὶ δίκην ἔριν, καὶ γινόμενα πάντα κατ' ἔριν καὶ χρεών.

Origen *Against Celsus.* The last phrase presumably means that the strife is a condition into which all things are driven by inner compulsion. Kirk (p. 242) offers the interpretation: "War-strife is everywhere, normal-course-of-events is war-strife, everywhere things happen by war-strife and normal-course-of-events."

Fr. 27 (D—; By 43). διὸ καὶ μέμφεται τῷ Ὁμήρῳ [Ἡράκλειτος] εἰπόντι· ὡς ἔρις ἔκ τε θεῶν ἔκ τ' ἀνθρώπων ἀπόλοιτο· οἰχήσεσθαι γάρ φησι πάντα.

Simplicius, in his commentary on Aristotle's *Categories*: published in *Commentaria in Aristotelem Graeca*, Vol. VIII, p. 412. Immediately before making the quotation Simplicius attributes to "the Heracliteans" the view that "if either of the opposites should fail, there would be complete and utter destruction of everything": εἰ γὰρ τὸ ἕτερον τῶν ἐναντίων ἐπιλείψει, οἴχοιτο ἂν πάντα ἀφανισθέντα. According to Aristotle (*Eudemian Ethics*, VII: 1235a, 26) Heraclitus supports his repudiation of Homer's remark by arguing that "there could be no harmony without both low and high notes, nor could life exist without both male and female." The Homeric reference is to *Iliad* xviii. 107.

Because of Simplicius' indirect way of introducing the quotation ("Heraclitus blames Homer for saying . . ."), a slight grammatical reconstruction has been necessary in the translation.

CHAPTER III. THE PROCESSES OF NATURE

Fr. 28 (D 90; By 22). πυρός τε ἀνταμοιβὴ τὰ πάντα καὶ πῦρ ἁπάντων ὅκωσπερ χρυσοῦ χρήματα καὶ χρημάτων χρυσός.

Plutarch *On the E at Delphi*, 388 E. Diels' rendering suggests a somewhat similar interpretation to the one here offered: "Umsatz findet wechselweise statt des Alls gegen das Feuer und des Feuers gegen das All. . . ." Kirk (p. 345) interprets somewhat differently: "All things are an equal exchange for fire and fire for all things. . . ." He justifies this by the statement that "ἀντ-reinforces the idea of exact reciprocity in ἀμοιβή" and he inter-prets the simile as emphasizing the equality of the exchanges. I would suggest that there might be a secondary connotation of moral repayment, or requital, in ἀνταμοιβή, as there is when Aeschylus uses forms of the verb ἀνταμείβεσθαι.

Fr. 29 (D 30; By 20). κόσμον τόνδε, τὸν αὐτὸν ἁπάντων, οὔτε τις θεῶν οὔτε ἀνθρώπων ἐποίησεν, ἀλλ᾽ ἦν ἀεὶ καὶ ἔστιν καὶ ἔσται, πῦρ ἀείζωον, ἁπτόμενον μέτρα καὶ ἀποσβεννύμενον μέτρα.

Clement *Stromata* II. 396. The two participles in the last clause should be taken in the middle voice, not in the passive; for Heraclitus does not think of the kindling and extinguishing as performed by any agency outside the fire itself.

There is a general ambiguity in the Fragment. Does it mean that the universe as a whole becomes fiery and becomes ex-tinguished at different times? At first sight the interpretation appears plausible, since the subject-accusative is κόσμον τόνδε. On this interpretation the word μέτρα would refer to regular periods of time, and Heraclitus would evidently be speaking of world-cycles. But since the question of whether he believed in the Stoic doctrine of world-cycles is a controversial one (dis-cussed in Chapter III), we ought to translate so as to avoid prejudging the controversy if possible. For it might be that μέτρα should be interpreted not temporally but quantitatively. That is, the word might refer to the degree to which the processes of kindling and extinguishing are constantly going on in the universe, while the universe itself remains an ever-living fire. Some such interpretation is made by those who wish to avoid ascribing the doctrine of world-cycles to Heraclitus. Such an interpretation would be consistent with the range of meaning of μέτρα and it might seem to be supported by the phrase πῦρ ἀείζωον, but I am unable to see how it can be consistent with the state-ment that the cosmos itself becomes kindled and extinguished. However, see Kirk's careful discussion of the probable meaning of κόσμος (pp. 314-324).

Fr. 30 (D 65; By 24). [καλεῖ δὲ αὐτὸ] χρησμοσύνην καὶ κόρον.

Hippolytus IX. Both Diels and Bywater limit the quotation to the words "craving and satiety." Nevertheless it is perfectly plain from Hippolytus' context that αὐτὸ refers to fire, and the meaning of the phrase is indeterminable unless the subject is specified. For in his *Refutatio* the present quotation is immediately preceded by the sentence, λέγει δὲ καὶ φρόνιμον τοῦτο εἶναι τὸ πῦρ καὶ τῆς διοικήσεως τῶν ὅλων αἴτιον.

Fr. 31 (D 91; By 40). σκίδνησι καὶ πάλιν συνάγει, καὶ πρόσεισι καὶ ἄπεισι.

Plutarch *On the E at Delphi* 392 C. In Plutarch this quotation follows the first clause of our Fr. 21, on the impossibility of stepping twice into the same river. Diels combines the two Fragments into his Fragment 91; but since they are apparently disparate in sense, and since Plutarch separates them by a few words of his own, I am presenting them here separately as Frs. 21 and 31. However, Plutarch evidently sees, or thinks he sees, a connection between them. After quoting Fr. 21 he continues: "Nor is it possible to lay hold twice of any mortal substance in a permanent state; by the suddenness and swiftness of the change in it there 'comes dispersion and, at another time, a gathering together'; or, rather, not at another time nor later, but at the same instant it both settles ino its place and forsakes its place; 'it is coming and going.'" (Translated by F. C. Babbitt, in his Loeb Classical Library edition of Plutarch, v, p. 241.) The two verbs in the first half of the Fragment are active and transitive.

Fr. 32 (D 31; By 21). πυρὸς τροπαὶ πρῶτον θάλασσα, θαλάσσης δὲ τὸ μὲν ἥμισυ γῆ, τὸ δὲ ἥμισυ πρηστήρ.

Clement *Stromata* II. 396.

Fr. 33 (D 31; By 23). θάλασσα διαχέεται, καὶ μετρέεται εἰς τὸν αὐτὸν λόγον ὁκοῖος πρόσθεν ἦν ἢ γενέσθαι γῆ.

Clement, *loc.cit.* Diels treats this as a continuation of Fr. 32. However, Clement quotes the two passages separately, with remarks of his own between, and the general similarity of subject matter does not prove that they stood together in Heraclitus' treatise.

Fr. 34 (D 76; By 25). ζῇ πῦρ τὸν γῆς θάνατον καὶ ἀὴρ ζῇ τὸν πυρὸς θάνατον, ὕδωρ ζῇ τὸν ἀέρος θάνατον, γῆ τὸν ὕδατος.

Maximus of Tyre, XLI. 4. Diels-Kranz retains only the first five and the last three words—evidently because of a supposed inconsistency with Fr. 32. See my discussion of this point in Chapter III. Cf. Plutarch, *On the E at Delphi*, 392 C.

Fr. 35 (D 64; By 28). τὰ δὲ πάντα οἰακίζει κεραυνός.

Hippolytus IX. In Fr. 120 κυβερνᾶτει replaces the present verb, evidently expressing the same idea.

Fr. 36 (D6; By 32). ὁ ἥλιος νέος ἐφ' ἡμέρῃ ἐστίν.

Aristotle *Meteorologica* 355 a, 14; confirmed by several other writers. A late writer Galenus (*Dox.*, p. 626) further explains that Heraclitus regarded the sun as a burning mass (ἄνεμμα), whose rising is a process of kindling (ἔξαψις) and whose setting is a process of quenching (σβέσις).

Fr. 37 (D 3; By —). [περὶ μεγέθους ἡλίου] εὖρος ποδὸς ἀνθρωπείου.

Aëtius, in *Dox.*, p. 351.

Fr. 38 (D 99; By 31). εἰ μὴ ἥλιος ἦν, ἕνεκα τῶν ἄλλων ἄστρων εὐφρόνη ἂν ἦν.

Plutarch quotes this in his essay, "Is Fire or Water the More Useful?" (957 A). The Greek idiom is a little odd: ἕνεκα τῶν ἄλλων ἄστρων εὐφρόνη ἂν ἦν does not mean "on account of the other stars it would be night"; for this makes no sense. The force of ἕνεκα is evidently weaker, and the indicated relation is about midway between the causal and the concessive; the idea being, "for all that the other stars could do. . . ." The word εὐφρόνη is a euphemism for "night."

Fr. 39 (D 120; By 30). ἠοῦς καὶ ἑσπέρας τέρματα ἡ ἄρκτος καὶ ἀντίον τῆς ἄρκτου οὖρος αἰθρίου Διός.

Strabo 1. i. 6.

Fr. 40 (D 124; By —). ὥσπερ σάρμα εἰκῆ κεχυμένων ὁ κάλλιστος [ὁ] κόσμος.

Theophrastus *Metaphysics* 15.

Fr. 41 (D 11; By 55). πᾶν [γὰρ] ἑρπετὸν πληγῇ νέμεται.

Pseudo-Aristotle *De Mundo* 401a, 11. The Aristotelian writer's preceding clause (καὶ φθείρεται τοῖς τοῦ θεοῦ πειθόμενα θεσμοῖς) indicates that he understands the quotation as referring to a divine blow.

CHAPTER IV. HUMAN SOUL

Fr. 42 (D 45; By 71). ψυχῆς πείρατα ἰὼν οὐκ ἂν ἐξεύροιο, πᾶσαν ἐπιπορευόμενος ὁδόν· οὕτω βαθὺν λόγον ἔχει.

Diogenes Laertius ix. 7. In *De Anima*, 11, Tertullian offers a somewhat shorter Latin version: "*Terminos animae nequaquam invenies omnem viam ingrediens.*"

Fr. 43 (D—; By—). [καὶ Ἡράκλειτος δὲ τὴν ἀρχὴν εἶναί φησι] ψυχήν [εἴπερ] τὴν ἀναθυμίασιν, ἐξ ἧς τἆλλα συνίστησιν. καὶ ἀσωματώτατόν τε καὶ ῥέον ἀεί· τὸ δὲ κινούμενον κινουμένῳ γινώσκεσθαι.

Aristotle *De Anima* 1: 405 a, 25-28. In the introductory clause Aristotle is probably giving his own philosophical inference as to what Heraclitus must have meant by his statement that soul is a fiery vaporization out of which everything else is derived. R. D. Hicks in his translation of *De Anima* renders ἀναθυμίασις simply as "vapor"; J. A. Smith in the Oxford translation renders it as "warm exhalation." The latter rendering has the double advantage of connoting process and of suggesting some affinity between this process and fire. I have chosen the phrase "fiery vaporization" as preserving both connotations and making the latter more explicit. The transformation from water to air (which the word "vaporization," applied to ancient Greek cosmology, would presumably denote) and the transformation from air to fire are conceived by Heraclitus as continuous aspects of the Upward Way—so continuous that (as observed in Chapter III) he sometimes finds it unnecessary to mention air as the intermediate state.

Neither Diels nor Bywater accepts the Fragment as a direct quotation from Heraclitus, and it must be admitted that several of the words have an Aristotelian ring. But while Aristotle may have employed a little freedom of language, he is seriously reporting what Heraclitus taught; and the contained ideas are too important to ignore.

Fr. 44 (D 12; By 41, 42). [καὶ] ψυχαὶ δὲ ἀπὸ τῶν ὑγρῶν ἀναθυμιῶνται.

Arius Didymus (*Dox.*, p. 471), where the sentence follows immediately after Fr. 21.

Fr. 45 (D 115; By —). ψυχῆς ἐστι λόγος ἑαυτὸν αὔξων.
Stobaeus *Florilegium* III. 1.

Fr. 46 (D 118; By 75). αὔη ψυχὴ σοφωτάτη καὶ ἀρίστη.

Stobaeus *Florilegium* III. 5, as given by Stephanus, followed by Walzer and others. Diels-Kranz accepts the reading, αὐγὴ ξηρὴ ψυχὴ. . . , which could be translated, "A soul which is a dry beam of light is wisest and best." But although the light imagery is quite in keeping with Heraclitus' style of thought, Burnet argues cogently (p. 138, n. 2) that the αὐγὴ ξηρὴ is a corruption.

Fr. 47 (D 77; By 72). ψυχῇσι τέρψιν [ἢ θάνατον] ὑγρῇσι γενέσθαι.

Numenius, by way of Porphyrius (*The Cave of the Nymphs* x). Here I follow Bywater's and Walzer's texts in omitting the two words as a probable interpolation. Diels-Kranz retains them, which would make the meaning "pleasure, which is to say death." It could be Heraclitus' own statement, but it sounds more like a copyist's attempt to make the implication explicit. In Porphyrius, and evidently in the writer from whom he quotes, the Fragment is followed by the statement, "They live in each other's death and die in each other's life," which in the present canon serves (on the authority of Hippolytus) as the second half of Fr. 66.

Fr. 48 (D 117; By 73). ἀνὴρ ὁκόταν μεθυσθῇ, ἄγεται ὑπὸ παιδὸς ἀνήβου σφαλλόμενος, οὐκ ἐπαΐων ὅκη βαίνει, ὑγρὴν τὴν ψυχὴν ἔχων.
Stobaeus *Florilegium* III. 5.—

Fr. 49 (D. 36; By 68). ψυχῇσιν θάνατος ὕδωρ γενέσθαι, ὕδατι δὲ θάνατος γῆν γενέσθαι, ἐκ γῆς δὲ ὕδωρ γίνεται, ἐξ ὕδατος δὲ ψυχή.
Clement *Stromata* II. 435. The first half of the quotation receives confirmation from Philo and Hippolytus.

Fr. 50 (D 125; By 84). καὶ ὁ κυκεὼν διίσταται μὴ κινούμενος.
Theophrastus *De Vertigine*, 9. The μὴ has been added by Bernays to the manuscript text, and is obviously needed.

Fr. 51 (D 85; By 105). θυμῷ μάχεσθαι χαλεπόν· ὃ γὰρ ἂν θέλῃ, ψυχῆς ὠνεῖται.
Plutarch *Life of Coriolanus* 224 C.

Fr. 52 (D 110; By 104). ἀνθρώποις γίνεσθαι ὁκόσα θέλουσιν οὐκ ἄμεινον.
Stobaeus *Florilegium* III. I.

Fr. 53 (D 95; By 108). ἀμαθίην [γὰρ] ἄμεινον κρύπτειν, ἔργον δὲ ἐν ἀνέσει καὶ παρ' οἶνον.
Plutarch *Quaestiones conviviales* 644 A.

Fr. 54 (D 87; By 117). βλὰξ ἄνθρωπος ἐπὶ παντὶ λόγῳ ἐπτοῆσθαι φιλεῖ.
Plutarch *On the Right Method of Hearing* 41 A.

Fr. 55 (D 34; By 3). ἀξύνετοι ἀκούσαντες κωφοῖσιν ἐοίκασι· φάτις αὐτοῖσιν μαρτυρεῖ παρεόντας ἀπεῖναι.
Clement *Stromata* II. 404.

Fr. 56 (D 46; By 132). τήν τε οἴησιν ἱερὰν νόσον [ἔλεγε καὶ τὴν ὅρασιν ψεύδεσθαι].
Diogenes Laertius IX. 7. According to Liddell and Scott οἴησις can mean either (or both) opinion or self-conceit; the word "bigotry" can perhaps convey the double connotation.

Fr. 57 (D 17; By 5). οὐ γὰρ φρονέουσι τοιαῦτα πολλοί, ὁκόσοι ἐγκυρεῦσιν, οὐδὲ μαθόντες γινώσκουσιν, ἑωυτοῖσι δὲ δοκέουσι.
Clement *Stromata* II. 117.

Fr. 58 (D 7; By 37). εἰ πάντα τὰ ὄντα καπνὸς γένοιτο, ῥῖνες ἂν διαγνοῖεν.
Aristotle *De Sensu* 443 a, 22. I translate ῥῖνες (literally "nostrils") as "smell," because obviously, since all things are now supposed to be smoke, the word must be intended metaphorically.

Fr. 59 (D 98; By 38). αἱ ψυχαὶ ὀσμῶνται καθ' Ἅιδην.

Plutarch *On the Face of the Moon* 943 D. The verb ὀσμῶνται means simply "smell," but the sense of the statement appears to be that this is how the souls of the dead, reduced to the condition of smoke, would have to perceive—an idea already indicated in the preceding Fragment.

Fr. 60 (D 96; By 85). νέκυες [γὰρ] κοπρίων ἐκβλητότεροι.

Plutarch *Quaestiones conviviales* 669 A; Strabo, XVI. iii. 26.

CHAPTER V. IN RELIGIOUS PERSPECTIVE

Fr. 61 (D 78; By 96). ἦθος [γὰρ] ἀνθρώπειον μὲν οὐκ ἔχει γνώμας, θεῖον δὲ ἔχει.

Origen *Against Celsus* VI. 12.

Fr. 62 (D —; By —). [καὶ μὴν ῥητῶς ὁ Ἡράκλειτός φησι] τὸ μὴ εἶναι λογικὸν τὸν ἄνθρωπον, μόνον δ᾽ ὑπάρχειν φρενῆρες τὸ περιέχον.

Sextus Empiricus *Adversus Mathematicos* VIII. 286; in the Loeb Classical Library edition. *Against the Logicians* II. 286 (in Vol. II of Sextus' writings). Although Diels and Bywater omit the Fragment from their lists, Sextus says that Heraclitus "expressly" (ῥητῶς) affirms it.

Fr. 63 (D 86; By 116). [ἀλλὰ] τῶν μὲν θείων τὰ πολλά [καθ᾽ Ἡράκλειτον] ἀπιστίῃ διαφυγγάνει μὴ γιγνώσκεσθαι.

Plutarch *Coriolanus* 232 D.

Fr. 64 (D 72; By 93). ᾧ μάλιστα διηνεκῶς ὁμιλοῦσι λόγῳ, τούτῳ διαφέρονται, [καὶ οἷς καθ᾽ ἡμέραν ἐγκυροῦσι, ταῦτα αὐτοῖς ξένα φαίνεται].

Marcus Aurelius IV. 46. I follow Burnet (p. 139, n. 3) in supposing that the bracketed words belong to Marcus Aurelius and not to Heraclitus.

Fr. 65 (D 26; By 77). ἄνθρωπος ἐν εὐφρόνῃ φάος ἅπτεται ἑαυτῷ· ἀποθανὼν ἀποσβεσθεὶς ὄψεις ζῶν δὲ ἅπτεται τεθνεῶτος εὕδων· ἀποσβεσθεὶς ὄψεις ἐγρηγορὼς ἅπτεται εὕδοντος.

Clement *Stromata* II. 310. Cf. Dindorf's ed., II, p. 399.

Of all the Fragments of Heraclitus there is none that has given rise to more textual disputes. Bywater, who appears to have gone on the principle of discarding every word that any scholar had disputed, gives a truncated version of the Fragment, which Fairbanks, following him, translates: "Man, like a light in the nighttime, is kindled and put out." Their interpretation loses the force of the complex pun on ἅπτεται, explained in Chapter v. The present version of the text is based partly on Diels-Kranz, partly on Dindorf's edition of Clement's *Stromata*; the two stops indicate what I take to be the main divisions of thought.

Fr. 66 (D 62; By 67). ἀθάνατοι θνητοί, θνητοὶ ἀθάνατοι, ζῶντες τὸν ἐκείνων θάνατον, τὸν δὲ ἐκείνων βίον τεθνεῶτες.

Hippolytus IX. Clement of Alexandria gives a different version: ἄνθρωποι θεοί, θεοὶ ἄνθρωποι (*Paedagogus* I. 236; cf. Dindorf, Vol. I, p. 326). Since "immortals" and "mortals" commonly meant, from Homer down, gods and men respectively, Clement's paraphrase is doubtless justified; however, the paradoxical form given by Hippolytus is more in keeping with Heraclitus' typical style. Moreover, supposing that the two Christian writers are referring to the same passage, it seems more likely that one of them should have undertaken to explain the meaning to his readers in literal terms than that the other should have taken a plain statement from Heraclitus and dressed it up as a paradox. Although no verb is specified in either version, the verb "become" (rather than "are") appears to be justified by the second half of the Fragment. Evidently Clement disagrees, since he adds the remark, λόγος γὰρ αὐτός, "for their meaning is the same."

Fr. 67 (D 27; By 122). ἀνθρώπους μένει ἀποθανόντας ἅσσα οὐκ ἔλπονται οὐδὲ δοκέουσιν.

Clement *Stromata* II. 312.

Fr. 68 (D 63; By 123). [ἔνθα δ' ἐόντι] ἐπανίστασθαι καὶ φύλακας γίνεσθαι ἐγερτὶ ζώντων καὶ νεκρῶν.

Hippolytus IX. The reference of "they" is uncertain.

Fr. 69 (D 119; By 121). ἦθος ἀνθρώπῳ δαίμων.

Stobaeus *Florilegium* IV. 40. Cf. also Plutarch *Moral Essays* 999 E.

Fr. 70 (D 25; By 101). μόροι [γὰρ] μέζονες μέζονας μοίρας λαγχάνουσι.

Clement *Stromata* II. 271. A pun on the somewhat different connotations of μόροι and μοίραι.

Fr. 71 (D 28; By 118). [καὶ μέντοι καὶ] Δίκη καταλήψεται ψευδῶν τέκτονας καὶ μάρτυρας.

Clement *Stromata* II. 331.

Fr. 72 (D 66; By 26). πάντα [γὰρ] τὸ πῦρ ἐπελθὸν κρινεῖ καὶ καταλήψεται.

Hippolytus IX. The last verb (future middle of καταλαμβάνειν), translated "will overtake" in Fr. 71 and here, could carry also the connotations of "catch by surprise" and "legally condemn."

Fr. 73 (D 16; By 27). τὸ μὴ δῦνόν ποτε πῶς ἄν τις λάθοι;

Clement *Paedagogia* I. 216.

Fr. 74 (D —; By —). εἶναι γὰρ καὶ ἐνταῦθα θεούς·

Aristotle *Parts of Animals* I. 5: 645 a, 17. The reference of the adverb was to a place by the stove, where some visitors unexpectedly found Heraclitus warming himself.

Fr. 75 (D 5; By 126). καὶ τοῖς ἀγάλμασι δὲ τουτέοισιν εὔχονται, ὁκοῖον εἴ τις δόμοισι λεσχηνεύοιτο, οὔ τι γινώσκων θεοὺς οὐδ᾽ ἥρωας οἵτινές εἰσι.

Aristarchus *Theosophia* 68; Origen *Against Celsus* VII. 62. In Aristarchus it follows Fr. 78; in Origen it stands alone. Diels-Kranz retains Aristarchus' coupling.

Fr. 76 (D 14; By 124, 125). νυκτιπόλοις, μάγοις, βάκχοις, λήναις, μύσταις. τὰ [γὰρ] νομιζόμενα κατ᾽ ἀνθρώπους μυστήρια ἀνιερωστὶ μυεῦνται.

Clement *Protrepticus* I. 16.

Fr. 77 (D 15; By 127). εἰ μὴ γὰρ Διονύσῳ πομπὴν ἐποιοῦντο καὶ ὕμνεον ᾆσμα αἰδοίοισιν, ἀναιδέστατα εἴργαστ᾽ ἄν· ὡυτὸς δὲ ᾽Αίδης καὶ Διόνυσος, ὅτεῳ μαίνονται καὶ ληναΐζουσιν.

Clement *Protrepticus* I. 26.

Fr. 78 (D 5; By 130). καθαίρονται δ᾽ ἄλλῳ αἵματι μιαινόμενοι οἷον εἴ τις εἰς πηλὸν ἐμβὰς πηλῷ ἀπονίζοιτο. μαίνεσθαι δ᾽ ἂν δοκοίη, εἴ τις αὐτὸν ἀνθρώπων ἐπιφράσαιτο οὕτω ποιέοντα.

Aristarchus *Theosophia*. See Note to Fr. 75.

Fr. 79 (D 92; By 12). Σίβυλλα δὲ μαινομένῳ στόματι ἀγέλαστα καὶ ἀκαλλώπιστα καὶ ἀμύριστα φθεγγομένη χιλίων ἐτῶν ἐξικνεῖται τῇ φωνῇ διὰ τὸν θεόν.

Plutarch *On the Pythian Oracles* 397 A.

CHAPTER VI. MAN AMONG MEN

Fr. 80 (D 113; By 91). ξυνόν ἐστι πᾶσι τὸ φρονέειν.

Stobaeus *Florilegium* III. i.

Fr. 81 (D 114; By 91). ξὺν νῷ λέγοντας ἰσχυρίζεσθαι χρὴ τῷ ξυνῷ πάντων, ὅκωσπερ νόμῳ πόλις, καὶ πολὺ ἰσχυροτέρως. τρέφονται γὰρ πάντες οἱ ἀνθρώπειοι νόμοι ὑπὸ ἑνὸς τοῦ θείου· κρατεῖ γὰρ τοσοῦτον ὁκόσον ἐθέλει καὶ ἐξαρκεῖ πᾶσιν καὶ περιγίνεται.

Stobaeus *Florilegium* III. 1. There is a play on words: ξὺν νῷ ("with rational awareness") and ξυνῷ ("to that which is common"). The pun is obscured by Diels-Kranz's reading of the second word as νόῳ. Here and in the last line I follow Walzer.

Fr. 82 (D 44; By 100). μάχεσθαι χρὴ τὸν δῆμον ὑπὲρ τοῦ νόμου ὅκωσπερ τείχεος.

Diogenes Laertius IX. 2.

Fr. 83 (D 33; By 110). νόμος καὶ βουλῇ πείθεσθαι ἑνός.

Clement *Stromata* II. 404.

Fr. 84 (D 49; By 113). εἰς ἐμοὶ μύριοι ἐὰν ἄριστος ᾖ.

Galenus. Cf. Symmachus via Walzer: "Heraclitum . . . *qui summam laudis arbitrabatur placere* UNI *si esset optimus.*"

Fr. 85 (D 29; By 111). αἱρεῦνται [γὰρ] ἓν ἀντὶ ἁπάντων οἱ ἄριστοι, κλέος ἀέναον θνητῶν· οἱ δὲ πολλοὶ κεκόρηνται ὅκωσπερ κτήνεα.

Clement *Stromata* II. 366.

Fr. 86 (D 24; By 102). ἀρηϊφάτους θεοὶ τιμῶσι καὶ ἄνθρωποι.

Clement *Stromata* II. 255.

Fr. 87 (D 28; By 118). δοκέοντα [γὰρ] ὁ δοκιμώτατος γινώσκει φυλάσσειν.

Clement *Stromata* II. 331. I follow the manuscript reading of the last word, which seems to me to make better sense than Diels-Kranz's arbitrary emendation.

Fr. 88 (D 43; By 103). ὕβριν χρὴ σβεννύναι μᾶλλον ἢ πυρκαϊήν.

Diogenes Laertius IX. 2.

Fr. 89 (D 84 b; By 82). κάματός ἐστι τοῖς αὐτοῖς μοχθεῖν καὶ ἄρχεσθαι.

Plotinus *Enneads* IV. 8, where it follows Fr. 23.

Fr. 90 (D 97; By 115). κύνες [γὰρ] καταβαΰζουσιν ὧν ἂν μὴ γινώσκωσι.

Plutarch *Whether Old Men Should Engage in Politics* 787 C.

Fr. 91 (D 104; By 111). τίς γὰρ αὐτῶν νόος ἢ φρήν; δήμων ἀοιδοῖσι πείθονται καὶ διδασκάλῳ χρείωνται ὁμίλῳ οὐκ εἰδότες ὅτι "οἱ πολλοὶ κακοί, ὀλίγοι δὲ ἀγαθοί."

Proclus, Commentary on Plato's *Alcibiades*, 1.

Fr. 92 (D 56; By —). ἐξηπάτηνται οἱ ἄνθρωποι πρὸς τὴν γνῶσιν τῶν φανερῶν παραπλησίως Ὁμήρῳ, ὃς ἐγένετο τῶν Ἑλλήνων σοφώτερος πάντων. ἐκεῖνόν τε γὰρ παῖδες φθεῖρας κατακτείνοντες ἐξηπάτησαν εἰπόντες· ὅσα εἴδομεν καὶ ἐλάβομεν, ταῦτα ἀπολείπομεν, ὅσα δὲ οὔτε εἴδομεν οὔτ' ἐλάβομεν, ταῦτα φέρομεν.

Hippolytus IX. The story is also told in the anonymous *De Vita Homeri* (falsely ascribed to Plutarch), Section 4.

Fr. 93 (D 42; By 119). τόν τε Ὅμερον ἄξιον ἐκ τῶν ἀγώνων ἐκβάλλεσθαι καὶ ῥαπίζεσθαι καὶ Ἀρχίλοχον ὁμοίως.

Diogenes Laertius IX. 1.

Fr. 94 (D 106; By 120). [Ἡράκλειτος ἐπέπληξεν] Ἡσιόδῳ τὰς μὲν ἀγαθὰς ποιουμένῳ τὰς δὲ φαύλας ὡς ἀγνοοῦντι φύσιν ἡμέρας ἀπάσας μίαν οὖσαν.

Plutarch *Camillus* 138 A. Seneca translates the content of the latter clause: *Unus dies par omni est* (*Epistles* XII. 7).

Fr. 95 (D 121; By 114). ἄξιον Ἐφεσίοις ἡβηδὸν ἀπάγξασθαι

πᾶσι καὶ τοῖς ἀνήβοις τὴν πόλιν καταλιπεῖν, οἵτινες Ἑρμόδωρον ἄνδρα ἑωυτῶν ὀνήιστον ἐξέβαλον φάντες· ἡμέων μηδὲ εἷς ὀνήιστος ἔστω, εἰ δὲ μή, ἄλλη τε καὶ μετ' ἄλλων.

Strabo XIV. i. 25 ; Diogenes Laertius IX. 2.

Fr. 96 (D 125a ; By —). μὴ ἐπιλίποι ὑμᾶς πλοῦτος, Ἐφέσιοι, ἵν' ἐξελέγχοισθε πονηρευόμενοι.

Tzetzes, in a commentary on Aristophanes, as quoted by Diels-Kranz and Walzer.

Fr. 97 (D 20; By 86). γενόμενοι ζώειν ἐθέλουσι μόρους τ' ἔχειν [μᾶλλον δὲ ἀναπαύεσθαι] καὶ παῖδας καταλείπουσι μόρους γενέσθαι.

Clement *Stromata* II. 201. Following Mullach and Walzer I regard the bracketed words as probably Clement's gloss.

CHAPTER VII. RELATIVITY AND PARADOX

Fr. 98 (D 8; By 46). τὸ ἀντίξουν συμφέρον καὶ ἐκ τῶν διαφερόντων καλλίστην ἁρμονίαν[, καὶ πάντα κατ' ἔριν γίνεσθαι].

Aristotle *Nicomachean Ethics* VIII:1155 b, I. On the translation of ἁρμονία(-η) see the note to Fr. 116.

Fr. 99 (D 111; By 104). νοῦσος ὑγιείην ἐποίησεν ἡδὺ καὶ ἀγαθόν, λιμὸς κόρον, κάματος ἀνάπαυσιν·

Stobaeus *Florilegium* III. I.

Fr. 100 (D 23; By 60). δίκης ὄνομα οὐκ ἂν ᾔδεσαν εἰ ταῦτα μὴ ἦν.

Clement *Stromata* II. 252.

Fr. 101 (D 61; By 52). θάλασσα ὕδωρ καθαρώτατον καὶ μιαρώτατον, ἰχθύσι μὲν πότιμον καὶ σωτήριον, ἀνθρώποις δὲ ἄποτον καὶ ὀλέθριον.

Hippolytus IX.

Fr. 102 (D 9; By 51). ὄνους σύρματ' ἂν ἑλέσθαι μᾶλλον ἢ χρυσόν.

Aristotle *Nicomachean Ethics* X. V: 1176 a, 8.

Fr. 103 (D 37; By 53). *Sues caeno, cohortales aves pulvere vel cinere lavari.*

Preserved in Latin by Columella VIII. 4.

Fr. 104 (D 82, 83; By 99, 98). πιθήκων ὁ κάλλιστος αἰσχρὸς ἀνθρώπων γένει συμβάλλειν· ἀνθρώπων ὁ σοφώτατος πρὸς θεὸν πίθηκος φανεῖται καὶ σοφίᾳ καὶ κάλλει καὶ τοῖς ἄλλοις πᾶσιν.

Plato *Hippias Major* 289 A-B. I have combined and treated as a single Fragment what both Diels-Kranz and Bywater list as separate quotations. In Socrates' discourse the two clauses are briefly separated, but apparently only to suit the conventions of conversation. Diels-Kranz prints the Fragment as a paraphrase rather than as a quotation, but accepts it as representing an opinion of Heraclitus. After the first clause Socrates adds the comparison: ". . . and the fairest pot is ugly compared with any maiden"; Lattimore ascribes this to Heraclitus, but most other scholars take it to be Socrates' addition.

Fr. 105 (D 79; By 97). ἀνὴρ νήπιος ἤκουσε πρὸς δαίμονος ὅκωσπερ παῖς πρὸς ἀνδρός.

Origen *Against Celsus* VI. 12. Diels-Kranz, Bywater, and most other scholars agree in taking πρός with accusative in Fr. 104 to indicate comparison with, but in Fr. 105 with the genitive to indicate a shift in point of view. The sense of δαίμων is at once vague and yet particular. Patrick's translation, "the Deity," is certainly wrong. Kathleen Freeman tries to steer between the universal and the particular by employing the word "divinity" without an article; Diels-Kranz says *"Gottheit"*; Walzer, *"il nume."*

Fr. 106 (D 102; By 61). τῷ μὲν θεῷ καλὰ πάντα καὶ ἀγαθὰ καὶ δίκαια, ἄνθρωποι δὲ ἃ μὲν ἄδικα ὑπειλήφασιν ἃ δὲ δίκαια.

Porphyrius *Quaestiones Homericae*, on Bk. IV of *The Iliad.* ·Both the definite article and the sense of the sentence show that the reference here is not to just any supernatural power, as in Frs. 104 and 105, but to the perspective that is universal and all-comprehensive.

Fr. 107 (D 58; By 58). οἱ [γοῦν] ἰατροί, τέμνοντες, καίοντες, [πάντῃ βασανίζοντες κακῶς τοὺς ἀρρωστοῦντας,] ἐπαιτέονται μηδὲν ἄξιοι μισθὸν λαμβάνειν [παρὰ τῶν ἀρρωστούντων].

Hippolytus IX. Although Diels-Kranz takes Hippolytus' next words, ταὐτὰ ἐργαζόμενοι, as part of the quotation, they strike me as belonging rather to Hippolytus' ensuing commentary.

Fr. 108 (D 60; By 69). ὁδὸς ἄνω κάτω μία καὶ ὡυτή.

Hippolytus IX. Cf. Tertullian *Adv. Marc.* II. 28: *"Quid enim ait Heraclitus ille tenebrosus? eadem via sursum et deorsum."*

Fr. 109 (D 103; By 70). ξυνὸν [γὰρ] ἀρχὴ καὶ πέρας ἐπὶ κύκλου [περιφερείας].

Porphyrius *Quaestiones Homericae*: on Bk. XIII of *The Iliad.* Diels-Kranz and Burnet accept the final word as a part of the quotation. On the other hand, since there is no other known instance of the word occurring in early Greek, other scholars have concluded that it is Porphyrius' addition. Wilamowitz (in *Hermes*, 62, p. 276) goes so far as to argue that the words ἐπὶ κύκλου should also be omitted—a procedure that had already been taken by Bywater in his text and by Fairbanks in his translation. But since both of the last two nouns of the manuscript version are in the genitive, it is possible to remove one of them alone. I have followed Gigon, p. 100, and Kirk, p. 113, in the present reading.

Fr. 110 (D 49a; By 81). ποταμοῖς τοῖς αὐτοῖς ἐμβαίνομέν τε καὶ οὐκ ἐμβαίνομεν· [εἰμέν τε καὶ οὐκ εἰμεν].

Quoted by the late Greek grammarian and allegorist named Heraclitus, who wrote a commentary on Homer. The bracketed words, which I take to be an addition by the doxographer, are accepted by Diels-Kranz and Burnet. On the other hand, Seneca's version of the Fragment (*Epistles* lviii. 23) is simply: "*In idem flumen bis descendimus et non descendimus.*" The word "bis" repeats the idea of Fr. 21 and may be omitted, since it does not appear in the Greek source just mentioned. Seneca adds, as his own explanation presumably: "*Manet enim idem fluminis nomen, aqua transmissa est.*" This seems more plausible than the Greek doxographer's interpretation.

Fr. 111 (D 59; By 50). γναφείῳ ὁδὸς εὐθεῖα καὶ σκολιὴ μία ἐστὶ καὶ ἡ αὐτή.

Hippolytus ix. He explains: "The circular movement of the instrument in the fuller's shop called 'the screw' is straight and curved, for it revolves up and circularly at the same time." Possibly this is what Heraclitus had in mind; but it may also be that he was playing upon the double meaning of εὐθύς, which can connote both "straight" and "right." Walzer is able to preserve the double connotation in Italian: "il percorso retto et curvo."

Fr. 112 (D 10; By 59). συνάψιες ὅλα καὶ οὐχ ὅλα, συμφερόμενον διαφερόμενον, συνᾷδον διᾷδον· [καὶ] ἐκ πάντων ἓν καὶ ἐξ ἑνὸς πάντα.

Pseudo-Aristotle *De Mundo* 396 b, 20.

Fr. 113 (D 88; By 78). ταὐτό [τ' ἔνι] ζῆν καὶ τεθνηκὸς καὶ [τὸ] ἐγρηγορὸς καὶ καθεῦδον καὶ νέον καὶ γηραιόν· τάδε γὰρ μεταπεσόντα ἐκεῖνά ἐστι κἀκεῖνα πάλιν μεταπεσόντα ταῦτα.

Plutarch *A Letter of Consolation to Apollonius* 106 E. The translation of μεταπεσόντα ταῦτα as "sudden unexpected reversal" seems to find some support in Kirk, who writes (p. 147); "That μεταπίπτειν is habitually used with this sense of sudden complete reversal is indicated especially by phrases like μετεπεπτώκει τὰ πράγματα (Lysias 20. 14; cf. Thucydides viii 68; Plato *Epistle* 7 325 A), meaning 'a revolution had occurred.' "

In making the first bracketed deletion I follow Wilamowitz (in *Hermes*, 62, p. 276); the second is more widely agreed upon.

Fr. 114 (D 57; By 35). διδάσκαλος δὲ πλείστων Ἡσίοδος·

τοῦτον ἐπίστανται πλεῖστα εἰδέναι, ὅστις ἡμέρην καὶ εὐφρόνην οὐκ ἐγίνωσκεν· ἔστι γὰρ ἕν.

Hippolytus ix. Cf. Hesiod, *Theogony*, 124 and 748.

Fr. 115 (D 48; By 66). τῷ οὖν τόξῳ ὄνομα βίος, ἔργον δὲ θάνατος.

From a Greek anonymous volume on Etymology which sets βίος as a heading. Whereas here the point of the word-play is left to the reader's imagination, in another version (in Eustathius' commentary on the *Iliad*) the pun between "bow" (βιός) and "life" (βίος) is made explicit.

VIII. THE HIDDEN HARMONY

Fr. 116 (D 54; By 47). ἁρμονίη ἀφανὴς φανερῆς κρείττων.

Hippolytus ix stated twice. How should ἁρμονίη be translated? Fairbanks, Freeman, and Lattimore translate it "harmony," but Burnet prefers "attunement," since the Greek word does not imply harmony in the presentday sense—i.e., simultaneous sounds, or chords. So much is true, but on the other hand two musicians whom I have consulted opposed the word "attunement" because it suggests to them the preparatory tuning up of the instruments. Kirk argues (p. 224) that ἁρμονίη, which had come from ἁρμόζειν ("to fit together"), probably did not yet have a musical significance in Heraclitus' day; accordingly he translates, "An unapparent connexion is stronger than an apparent." Nevertheless, it is clear that Heraclitus intends a cosmic, archetypal significance, and it appears to me that this is better suggested by our word "harmony" than by any English alternative. The same argument applies to Fr. 117.

Fr. 117 (D 51; By 45). οὐ ξυνιᾶσιν ὅκως διαφερόμενον ἑωυτῷ ὁμολογέει· παλίντροπος ἁρμονίη ὅκωσπερ τόξου καὶ λύρης.

Hippolytus ix. Bywater offers as a separate fragment (No. 56 in his list) Plutarch's version of the statement (*On a Tranquil Mind* 473 F—474 A) where the name of Heraclitus is not mentioned. The important difference among these several versions of the aphorism is that whereas Hippolytus records the word παλίντροπος ("bending back"), Plutarch gives in its place the word παλίντονος ("inverse harmony"), both in the essay just mentioned and in his essay *On Isis and Osiris*, 369 B. Of course there may possibly have been two separate passages in Heraclitus' treatise, each employing one of the words, as Bywater evidently supposes. But in making a choice I think it best to follow Diels-Kranz and Fairbanks in accepting παλίντροπος instead of Burnet, Walzer, and Kirk in accepting παλίντονος. Psychologically it appears more likely that there might have been a shift from the first word to the second, stimulated by the musical simile that follows, than in the opposite direction. Cf. Plato *Symposium* 187 A.

Fr. 118 (D 50; By 1). οὐκ ἐμοῦ ἀλλὰ τοῦ λόγου ἀκούσαντας ὁμολογεῖν σοφόν ἐστιν ἓν πάντα εἶναι.

Hippolytus ix. Burnet's translation, "not to me, but to my Word," does not strike me as making good sense. It obscures the intended contrast, which is between the personal and the suprapersonal. Adolf Busse, however, argues in favor of Burnet's interpretation, in his essay, "Der Wortsinn von Logos bei Heraklit," in *Rheinisches Museum*, 75 (1926), pp. 203ff. Busse points out that it was customary with the Greeks, "as often with Plato," to distinguish between oneself and the word which one speaks. Accordingly he translates λόγος in this instance as *Wahrheitsbeweis*, adding parenthetically "(die Stimme der Wahrheit)." But Busse agrees that in Frs. 1 and 2 the primary reference is to the cosmic aspect; and there he renders λόγος as *Weltgesetz*.

Bruno Snell, in *Hermes*, 61, p. 365, argues along somewhat similar lines, stressing the connotation of "meaning" (*meinen*) in the words λόγος and λέγειν. "Logos," according to him, refers to the real meaning of Heraclitus' words, and thus may be distinguished from the words themselves with their accidental and personal characteristics. It is as if one were to say: "Don't merely listen to me, and to the sounds I make; attend rather to the meaning which they are intended to express."

As for the word ὁμολογεῖν, Kirk offers the view (pp. 67-68) that it contains a deliberate word-play. He argues that just as λόγος means something much more than "word," so ὁμολογεῖν means more than "say the same word" or "agree," although it carries this sense too. But it also carries the connotation of being in agreement with the Logos, of not opposing the Logos by refusing to listen to it. Added weight is doubtless given to Kirk's theory by the use of the word which Hippolytus makes directly after the quotation: καὶ ὅτι τοῦτο οὐκ ἴσασιν πάντες οὐδὲ ὁμολογεοῦσιν, ἐπιμέμφεται ὡδέ πως . . .

Fr. 119 (D 32; By 65). ἓν τὸ σοφὸν μοῦνον, λέγεσθαι οὐκ ἐθέλει καὶ ἐθέλει Ζηνὸς ὄνομα.

Clement *Stromata* ii. 404. The comma is not found in the manuscript, but is evidently required by the sense.

Fr. 120 (D 41; By 19). ἐν [γὰρ] τὸ σοφόν, ἐπίστασθαι γνώμην ὅπη κυβερνᾶται πάντα διὰ πάντων.

Diogenes Laertius IX. I. The verb κυβερνᾶται can be taken as either middle or passive in voice—as meaning "steer themselves" or as "are steered." Probably the distinction was not yet explicit in Heraclitus' mind and vocabulary. Walzer writes "si governa"; but the middle voice in Italian has a more nearly impersonal connotation than in English.

For the variants of ὅπη, See Walzer, p. 80.

Fr. 121 (D 67; By 36). ὁ θεὸς ἡμέρη εὐφρόνη, χειμὼν θέρος, πόλεμος εἰρήνη, κόρος λιμός, ἀλλοιοῦται δὲ ὅκωσπερ < > ὁπόταν συμμιγῆ θυώμασιν, ὀνομάζεται καθ᾽ ἡδονὴν ἑκάστου.

Hippolytus IX. The triangular brackets indicate the probable place of the main noun, missing from the manuscript. Since it was evidently dropped out by a copyist, there is no clue as to its nature or length. Several interpreters, including Diels-Kranz, Burnet, and Lattimore, have supplied the word "fire," and Burnet accordingly offers the translation, ". . . just as fire, when it is mingled with spices, is named according to the savor of each." There is no textual support for the interpretation.

Among the other conjectures that have been offered are: "wine" (Schuster), "olive oil" (Snell), and "air" (Zeller). There is no textual support for any of them, and in my text and translation I have employed triangular brackets in order to avoid prejudging the question. Actually I am most inclined to agree with Hermann Fränkel's theory, developed in his article, "Heraclitus on God and the Phenomenal World" (see Appendix D, Pt. 3) and outlined in Chapter VIII—namely, that Heraclitus may have been drawing a comparison with the ancient practice of manufacturing unguents by blending a pure oily base with a concentrated odoriferous extract. On this hypothesis, the missing word would mean something like "neutral base" (oily, or possibly waxen), and θύωμα would not mean either "incense" or "spices" (as various translators have interpreted it) but "scent" or "fragrance." Cf. Plato Timaeus 50 C: "A substance that receives all bodies (σώματα) must itself be pure."

Fr. 122 (D 94; By 29). ἥλιος [γὰρ] οὐχ ὑπερβήσεται μέτρα· εἰ δὲ μή, Ἐρινύες μιν Δίκης ἐπίκουροι ἐξευρήσουσιν.

Plutarch On Exile 604 A. The same idea with slight verbal differences is found in Plutarch's On Isis and Osiris 370 D; here the handmaids are characterized as "stern-eyed" (γοργῶπάς . . . ἐπικούρους) and the term "Erinyes" is omitted.

Fr. 123 (D 100; By 34). ὧρας [αἱ] πάντα φέρουσι.
Plutarch *Platonic Inquiries* 1007 D.

Fr. 124 (D 75; By 90). καὶ τοὺς καθεύδοντας ἐργάτας εἶναι καὶ συνεργοὺς τῶν ἐν τῷ κόσμῳ γινομένων.
Marcus Aurelius VI. 42.

MAIN DOXOGRAPHICAL SOURCES

(Numbers refer to the Fragments. Consult the Index for writers not here mentioned.)

Aristotle and his school: 20, 27, 36, 41, 43, 44, 58, 74, 98, 102, 112.

Clement of Alexandria: 3, 4, 16, 19, 21, 29, 32, 33, 49, 55, 57, 65, 67, 70, 71, 73, 76, 77, 83, 85, 86, 87, 97, 100, 119.

Diels, *Doxographi Graeci*: 37, 44.

Diogenes Laertius: 5, 6, 42, 56, 82, 88, 93, 120.

Hippolytus: 11, 24, 25, 30, 35, 66, 68, 72, 92, 101, 107, 108, 111, 114, 116, 117, 118, 121.

Marcus Aurelius: 14, 64, 124.

Maximus of Tyre: 34.

Origen: 26, 61, 75, 105.

Plato: 20, 104.

Plotinus: 23, 89.

Plutarch: 8, 15, 18, 21, 28, 31, 38, 51, 53, 54, 59, 60, 63, 79, 90, 94, 113, 122, 123.

Polybius: 12.

Porphyrius: 47, 106, 109.

Proclus: 17, 91.

Sextus Empiricus: 1, 2, 13, 62.

Stobaeus: 7, 9, 10, 45, 46, 48, 52, 69, 80, 81, 99.

Strabo: 39, 60, 95.

Theophrastus: 40, 50.

APPENDIX C

DISCARDED FRAGMENTS

The Fragments that follow are included in the Diels-Kranz list, but are omitted from the chapters of the present volume, as being either too trivial or obscure or insufficiently authorized to be of use in reconstructing the philosophy of Heraclitus.

Fr. 125 (D 4; By —). *If happiness consisted in bodily pleasures, we would describe cattle as happy when they are eating fodder.* Not found earlier than Albertus Magnus, in Latin translation.

Fr. 126 (D 13; By 54). *To delight in mud.* βορβόρῳ χαίρειν. Athenagoras quotes these two words from Heraclitus, with the implication that Heraclitus, like himself, means that it is something to be avoided. But there is not enough basis here for a full quotation. Cf. Fr. 103.

Fr. 127 (D 19; By 6). *Not knowing how to listen or how to speak.* The subject of the sentence in Heraclitus is not stated.

Fr. 128 (D 40; By 16). *Otherwise it would have taught Hesiod and Pythagoras, Xenophanes and Hectaeus.* A continuation of Fr. 6, in Diogenes Laertius as well as in Diels-Kranz and Bywater. But since Fr. 6 contributes to the topic of Chapter 1 whereas the present clause does not, it has seemed best to separate them. Moreover, the clause is added only by Diogenes Laertius; omitted by Clement of Alexandria and Aulus Gellius. See note to Fr. 6.

Fr. 129 (D 38; By 33). *The first to study astronomy.* According to Diogenes Laertius, Heraclitus said this about Thales.

Fr. 130 (D 39; By 112). *Bias of Pirene, son of Tutamas, is of far greater account than the rest.* Diogenes Laertius. Nothing else is known about Bias.

Fr. 131 (D 68; By 129). *Remedies.* The rites of the Mysteries, although shameful, are described by Heraclitus as "remedies" (Iamblichus *De Mysteriis* I. 11). No doubt an interesting doctrine of Heraclitus' psychology may lurk here, but since only one word is quoted there is nothing solid on which to build a conjecture.

Fr. 132 (D 69; By 128). Iamblichus (*De Mysteriis* v. 15) says that Heraclitus distinguishes two kinds of sacrifices: those which are performed by men who have first purified themselves and those performed in an ordinary way. But Diels-Kranz takes the words to be those of Iamblichus, not of Heraclitus; while Burnet rejects the passage altogether.

Fr. 133 (D 70; By —). *Children's toys.* According to Iamblichus, *De Anima*, Heraclitus so characterizes men's conjectures.

✕ Fr. 134 (D 71; By —). *He who forgets where the road leads.* Marcus Aurelius (*Meditations* IV. 46) says we should take note of such a man. He is evidently quoting Heraclitus' phrase from memory, and there is no way of knowing how Heraclitus himself employed it.

Fr. 135 (D 74; By —). *Like children to their parents.* From Marcus Aurelius' reference (*op.cit.*) it appears that Heraclitus employed the phrase negatively, in warning against an attitude of uncritical acceptance.

Fr. 136 (D 81; By —). *Leader of those who wrangle.* Heraclitus may have applied the phrase to Pythagoras, or to some group in the Pythagorean school.

Fr. 137 (D 105; By—). *Homer was an astrologer.*

Fr. 138 (D 122; By 9). *Approximations.*

APPENDIX D

BIBLIOGRAPHY

1. BASIC SOURCES

The two standard lists of Fragments, to one or the other of which nearly all scholarly references have been made during the last half century, are those of Bywater and Diels, the latter having been later revised by Kranz. The full titles of these three volumes (Bywater, Diels, and Diels-Kranz) will be found in Section 2 of the Bibliography. The Fragments as understood and translated in the present volume follow Diels-Kranz except where otherwise noted in Appendix B. Walzer's collection of the Fragments in Greek and Italian is likewise listed in Section 2 of the Bibliography; but this collection should also be mentioned here because of its unusual value in supplying, in addition to the text of the Fragments, the doxographical context in which it appears, i.e., the sentences preceding and following it in the ancient writers from whom a given Fragment is quoted. Thus both Diels-Kranz and Walzer, although strictly speaking they are secondary sources, have served me, as they have served many another worker in the field, virtually in the capacity of primary sources; for they provide a number of ancient materials, which might have been overlooked in going to the ancient sources alone, as well as a few quotations from rarely found authors who would otherwise have been difficult of access.

My references to Aristotle's *De Anima* are to the edition and translation (Greek and English) of R. D. Hicks (Cambridge University Press, 1907). For the *Metaphysics* I have used the W. D. Ross edition (Oxford, 1924). For other parts of Aristotle I have employed the Loeb Classical Library edition, supplemented by the Oxford University Press translations under the general editorship of Sir David Ross.

Plato, Hippocrates, Diogenes Laertius, Plutarch, and Sextus Empiricus are quoted or translated from the Loeb Classical Library editions of their writings. Sometimes the translations of these editions have been employed, sometimes the passages have been translated anew. In the case of Plato, Cornford's translation of and commentary on the *Theaetetus* and *Sophist* were also used: Francis M. Cornford, *Plato's Theory of Knowledge* (Humanities Press, 1935; Liberal Arts Press, 1957).

The quotations from Heraclitus made by Hippolytus (the most valuable group from a single doxographical source that we possess) are all to be found in Book ix of *The Refutation of All Heresies*. The following editions of this work were used:

Hippolytus, *Philosophumena, sive Haeresitum Omnium Confutatio*. Greek text ed. by Patrice Cruice with Latin translation (Paris, 1860).

Hippolytus, *Philosophumena, or Refutation of All Heresies*. Eng. tr. by F. Legge (London, 1921).

Clement of Alexandria *Opera* edited by Otto Stahlin, in *Die griechischen christlichen Schriftsteller der ersten drei Jahrhunderte* (Leipzig, 1905-1909; 3 vols. in four).

Quotations from the late Greek doxographers Aëtius, Arius Didymus, and Galenus are taken from Hermann Diels, *Doxographi Graeci* (Berlin, 1879, 1929).

Quotations from the Greek commentators on Aristotle—Alexander Aphrodisiensis, Asclepius, and Simplicius—have been taken from Volumes i, vi, and vii respectively of *Commentaria in Aristotelem Graeca* (Berlin, 1882-1907).

Stobaeus: as cited by Diels and Walzer, *op.cit.*

2. COLLECTIONS AND TRANSLATIONS

The first collection of Heraclitus' Fragments was made by Friedrich Schleiermacher in 1817, and the text of each Fragment was accompanied by a German translation and an expository discussion. Although Schleiermacher's list has subsequently been amplified and superseded, it is of unique historical importance: all later lists have stemmed from it, directly or indirectly, and moreover it made Heraclitus available to nineteenth century philosophers and poets in something like an integral form. Goethe and Nietzsche were both deeply influenced by its contents. Schuster's list, published in German in 1873, added a number of important Fragments to those collected by Schleiermacher, and for three decades thereafter it was the list to which most German workers in the field were likely to appeal. The main collections of Fragments since that time, listed chronologically, are as follows. For the sake of easy reference the name of the editor or translator in each case precedes the title, regardless of sequence on the title-page. The asterisk (*) indicates works of primary importance.

Schleiermacher, Friedrich, *Herakleitos der Dunkle von Ephesos*: in his *Werke*, 3. Abteilung, 2. Band, pp. 1-146.

*Bywater, Ingram: *Heracliti Ephesi Reliquiae* (Oxford, 1877). Greek text and notes. Bywater attempts a loosely topical arrangement.

Mullach, Friedrich Wilhelm: *Fragmenta Graecorum Philosophorum* (Paris, 1883-1888). Greek text and Latin translation of the early Greek philosophers.

Patrick, G. T. W.: *The Fragments of the Work of Heraclitus of Ephesus on Nature* (Baltimore, 1889). English translation and introductory essay, the Greek text being supplied in an Appendix.

*Burnet, John: *Early Greek Philosophy* (London, 1892; third edition, 1920). My references are to the 1952 reprint of the third edition. Chapter III is devoted to Heraclitus; Burnet's translation of the Fragments is based upon Bywater's arrangement, but with independent judgments as to authenticity and interpretation.

*Fairbanks, Arthur: *The First Philosophers of Greece* (London, 1898). Pp. 23-63 are devoted to Heraclitus. Greek text and English translation of the Fragments, based on Bywater's arrangement.

Diels, Hermann: *Herakleitos von Ephesos* (Berlin, 1901). Greek text, German translation; a forerunner of the Heraclitus material in the volume that follows.

*Diels, Hermann: *Die Fragmente der Vorsokratiker* (Berlin, 1903; 3 volumes). In the fourth edition of this work (1922), the last edition for which Diels himself was responsible before his death, pp. 67-113 of Volume I are devoted to Heraclitus. Diels' "A" list comprises ancient statements about Heraclitus and his philosophy; the "B" list consists of what Diels judges to be authentic quotations, given in Greek text and German translation. Diels arranges his Fragments, except for the first two, which according to Sextus Empiricus had stood at the head of Heraclitus' treatise, according to the alphabetically ordered names of the ancient authors who have preserved them by quoting them.

Bordrero, Emilio: *Eraclito* (Turin, 1910). Italian translation with discussion.

Stöhr, Adolf: *Heraklit* (Leipzig, 1920). Greek text and German translation.

Burckhardt, Georg: *Heraklit, seine Gestalt und sein Künden* (Zurich, 1925). Greek text and German translation. Re-edited (Wiesbaden, 1951) with the title, *Heraklit, Urworte der Philosophie.*

Snell, Bruno: *Heraklit, Fragmente* (Munich, 1926). Greek text and German translation.

Solovine, Maurice: *Héraclite d'Ephèse* (Paris, 1931). French translation.

Jones, W. H. S.: "Heraclitus on the Universe," in Volume IV of the Works of Hippocrates (Loeb Classical Library, 1931). Greek text and English translation.

*Diels, Hermann and Kranz, Walther: Diels, *Die Fragmente der Vorsokratiker,* revised by Walther Kranz (Berlin, 1934). Published as the fifth edition of Diels' work; but while it retains Diels' numbering of the Fragments, it often alters his translations and sometimes his text in important respects. Abbreviated "Diels-Kranz."

Lattimore, Richmond: on pp. 119-128 of Matthew T. McClure, *The Early Philosophers of Greece* (New York, 1935). The translation of the Fragments, following Bywater's arrangement, by Lattimore; the ensuing discussion by McClure.

*Walzer, Richard: *Eraclito; Raccolta dei frammenti e traduzione italiana* (Florence, 1939). Greek text, Italian translation; together with Greek texts of passages from ancient authors supplying different versions of the Fragments. Follows Diels' arrangement.

Gaos, José: *Heráclito* (Mexico City, 1939). Spanish translation.

Mazzantini, C.: *Eraclito* (Turin, 1945). Greek text, Italian translation.

Freeman, Kathleen: *Ancilla to the Pre-Socratic Philosophers* (Oxford, 1948). English translation of Heraclitus' Fragments, pp. 24-34, following Diels.

Battistini, Yves: *Héraclite d'Ephèse* (Paris, 1948). French translation.

Kirk, G. S.: *Heraclitus, the Cosmic Fragments* (Cambridge, 1954). Text and translation, in doxographical context, of 45 of the Fragments.

Quiring, Heinrich: *Heraklit; Worte tönen durch Jahrtausende* (Berlin, 1959). Greek text, German translation.

3. BOOKS ON HERACLITUS

Aurobindo, Sri, *Heraclitus* (Calcutta, 1941). In English. Generally catalogued in libraries under the name "Ghose," which however is not used in Sri Aurobindo's published writings.

Bernays, Jacob, *Gesammelte Abhandlungen*, Vol. 1 (Berlin, 1885). The first volume consists of articles on Heraclitus.

Bernays, Jacob, *Die heraklitischen Briefe* (Berlin, 1869). Although the letters which Diogenes Laertius ascribes to Heraclitus are admittedly spurious, Bernays approaches them guided by the question, "What kind of evidence can be obtained from spurious writings?"

Bise, Pierre, *La politique d'Héraclite d'Ephèse* (Paris, 1925).

Brecht, J., *Heraklit; ein Versuch über den Ursprung der Philosophie* (Heidelberg, 1936).

Cuppini, Noemi, *Esposizione del sistema di Eraclito* (Rome, 1912).

Dauriac, Lionel, *De Heraclito Ephesio* (Paris, 1878).

Frankian, Aram M., *Héraclite*. Appears as Vol. 1 of the author's *Etudes de philosophie présocratique* (Paris, 1933).

Gigon, Olof, *Untersuchungen zu Heraklit* (Leipzig, 1935).

Gladisch, August, *Herakleitos und Zoroaster* (Leipzig, 1859).

Gomperz, Theodor, *Zu Heraklits Lehre und den Ueberresten seines Werkes* (Vienna, 1887).

Herr, Alfred, *Beiträge zur Exegese der Fragmente des Herakleitos von Ephesos* (Eger, 1912).

*Kirk, G. S., *Heraclitus, the Cosmic Fragments* (Cambridge, Eng., 1952). The most important book on Heraclitus that has appeared in English.

Kirk, William C., *Fire in the Cosmological Speculations of Heraclitus* (Minneapolis, 1940; Princeton Ph.D. thesis).

Lassalle, Ferdinand, *Die Philosophie Herakleitos des Dunklen von Ephesus*, 2 vols. (Berlin, 1858). Also published as Vols. VII-VIII of his *Gesammelte Reden und Schriften* (1919-1920).

Macchioro, Vittorio, *Eraclito; nuovi studi sull'orfismo* (Bari, 1922).

Mayer, G., *Heraklit von Ephesus und Arthur Schopenhauer* (Heidelberg, 1886).

Mohr, J., *Heraklitische Studien* (Zweibrücken, 1886).

Patin, Alois, *Heraklits Einheitslehre* (Leipzig, 1866).

Patin, Alois, *Quellenstudien zu Heraklit; pseudohippokratische Schriften* (Würzburg, 1881).

Pfleiderer, Edmund, *Die Philosophie des Heraklit von Ephesus im Lichte der Mysterienidee* (Berlin, 1886).

Pressley, G., *Die metaphysischen Anschauungen Heraklits von Ephesus* (Magdeburg, 1908).

Rivier, André, *Un emploi archaïque de l'analogie chez Héraclite et Thucydide.* (Lausanne, 1952).

Schäfer, G., *Die Philosophie des Heraklit von Ephesus und die moderne Heraklitforschung* (Leipzig, 1902).

Schultz, Wolfgang, *Pythagoras und Heraklit* (Leipzig, 1905). Published as Vol. 1 of his *Studien zur antiken Kultur* (Leipzig, 1905-1907).

Schuster, P., *Heraklit von Ephesus* (Leipzig, 1873).

Sloninsky, H., *Heraklit und Parmenides*, published as Vol. vii, Heft 1, of *Philosophische Arbeiten*, edited by Hermann Cohen and Paul Natorp (Giessen, 1912).

Spengler, Oswald, *Der metaphysische Grundgedanke der heraklitischen Philosophie* (Halle, 1904).

Spengler, Osvaldo, *Heráclito* (Buenos Aires, 1947). The first half of the volume consists of a long essay by Rodolfo Mondolfo discussing the views of eleven other Heraclitean scholars. There follows a Spanish translation by Augusta de Mondolfo of Spengler's aforementioned essay.

Surig, Henrik Wilhelm, *De Betekenis van Logos bij Herakleitos volgens de Traditie en de Fragmenten* (Nijmegen, 1951). With a summary in English and an extensive bibliography.

Teichmüller, Gustave, *Herakleitos*: Vol. 1 of his *Neue Studien zur Geschichte der Begriffe* (Gotha, 1876-1879).

Weerts, Emil, *Heraklit und Herakliteer* (Berlin, 1926).

4. ARTICLES ON HERACLITUS

Auerbach, Walter, "Zur Gegenüberstellung von Sein und Schein bei Heraklit," *Eos*, 33 (1930), pp. 651-664.

———, "De principio heraclito," *Eos*, 32 (1929), pp. 301-314.

Binswanger, Ludwig, "Heraklits Auffassung des Menschen," *Die Antike*, 11 (1935), pp. 1-39.

Brieger, A., "Die Grundzüge der heraklitischen Physik," *Hermes*, 39 (1904), pp. 182-223.

Busse, Adolf, "Der Wortsinn von Logos bei Heraklit," *Rheinisches Museum*, 75 (1926), pp. 203ff.

Calogero, Guido, "Eraclito," *Giornale critico di filosifia italiana,* 1936, pp. 195-224.

Capelle, W., "Das erste Fragment des Herakleitos," *Hermes,* 59 (1924), pp. 190-203.

Cataudella, Q., "L'armonia invisibile di Eraclito," *Sophia,* 17 (1949), pp. 332-333, On Fr. 116.

Cherniss, Harold, review of Olof Gigon, *Untersuchungen zu Heraklit, American Journal of Philology,* 56 (1935), pp. 414-416.

Deichgräber, Karl, "Bemerkungen zu Diogenes' Bericht über Heraklit," *Philologus,* 93 (1938), pp. 12-30.

Diels, Hermann, "Heraclitus," *Hastings' Encyclopaedia of Religion and Ethics,* 6, pp. 591-594.

Disandro, C. A., "Heráclito y el Lenguaje," *Revue de Argué,* 3 (1954).

Fiore Sole, G., "Il problema di Dio in Eraclito ed Eschilo," *Sophia,* 16 (1948), pp. 203-205, 357-361.

Fränkel, Hermann, "Heraclitus on God and the Phenomenal World," *American Philological Association, Proceedings,* 69 (1938), pp. 230-244.

——, "Heraclitus on the Notion of Generation," *American Journal of Philology,* 59 (1938), pp. 89-91.

——, "A Thought Pattern in Heraclitus," *American Journal of Philology,* 59 (1938), pp. 309-337.

——, German version of his articles on Heraclitus, in his *Dichtung und Philosophie des frühen Griechentums* (New York, 1938), pp. 474-505.

Friedländer, Paul, "Herakliti Frag. 124," *American Journal of Philology,* 63 (1942), p. 336. This is our Fr. 40.

Glasson, T. F., "Heraclitus' Alleged Logos Doctrine," *Journal of Theological Studies,* 3 (London, 1952), pp. 231-238.

Gomperz, Heinrich, "Ueber die ursprüngliche Reihefolge einiger Bruchstücke Heraklits," *Hermes,* 58 (1923), pp. 20-56.

Gregoire, F., "Héraclite et les cultes enthousiastes," *Revue néoscholastique de philosophie,* 38 (Louvain, 1935), pp. 43-63.

Heidegger, Martin, "Heraklit," 'Αντίδορον. *Festschrift zur Feier des 350jahrigen Bestands des Heinrich-Suso-Gymnasiums in Konstanz* (1954).

——, "Logos," *Vorträge und Aufsätze,* pp. 207-230.

Hoelscher, U., "Der Logos bei Heraklit," *Festschrift für Karl Reinhardt* (Cologne, 1952).

Howald, E., "Heraklit und seine antiken Beurteiler," *Neue Jahrbücher für die klassischen Altertümer*, 27 (1918).

Kerschensteiner, Jula, "Der Bericht des Theophrast über Heraklit," *Hermes*, 83 (1955), pp. 385-411.

Kirk, G. S., "Heraclitus and Death in Battle," *American Journal of Philology*, 70 (1949), pp. 384-393.

——, "Natural Change in Heraclitus," *Mind*, 60 (1951), pp. 35-42.

Kranz, Walther, "Der Logos Heraklits und der Logos des Johannes," *Rheinisches Museum*, 93 (1949), pp. 81-95.

Leuze, O., "Zu Heraklit Frag. 26 (Diels)," *Hermes*, 50 (1915), pp. 604-625. This is our Fr. 65.

Loew, Emmanuel, "Heraklit von Ephesus: die Entstehung des empirisch-physikalischen Wegens der Forschung," *Rheinisches Museum*, 79 (1930), pp. 123-152.

——, "Heraklit im Kampfe gegen den Logos," *Archiv zur Geschichte der Philosophie*, 23 (1910), pp. 89-91.

——, "Das heraklitische Wirklichkeitsproblem und seine Umdeutung bei Sextus," *Jahresbericht des Sophiengymnasiums in Wien* (1914).

——, "Das Lehrgedicht des Parmenides eine Kampfschrift gegen die Lehre Heraklits," *Rheinisches Museum*, 79 (1930), pp. 209-214.

——, "Parmenides und Heraklit im Wechselkampfe," *Archiv zur Geschichte der Philosophie*, 24 (1911), pp. 343-369.

——, "Das Verhältnis von Lehre und Logik bei Heraklit," *Wiener Studien*, 51 (1933), pp. 14-30.

——, "Die Zweiteilung in der Terminologie Heraklits," *Archiv zur Geschichte der Philosophie*, 24 (1911), pp. 1-21.

Maddalena, A., "Eraclito nell'interpretazione di Plato e d'Aristotele," *Atti dell'Istituto Veneto di Scienze, Lettere ed Arti*, 98 (Venice, 1938-1939), pp. 309-335.

Merlan, Philip, "Ambiguity in Heraclitus," *Actes du XIème congrès international de philosophie*, 12 (1953), 56-60.

——, "Heraclitus fr. B93D," *American Philological Association, Transactions and Proceedings*, 80 (1949), p. 429. This is our Fr. 18.

Minar, F. L., "The Logos of Heraclitus," *Classical Philology*, 34 (1939), pp. 323ff.

Mondolfo, Rodolfo, "Evidence of Plato and Aristotle relating to the *ekpyrosis* of Heraclitus," *Phronesis*, 3 (1958), pp. 75-82.

Muth, R., "Herakleitos, I. Bericht: 1939 bis 1953," *Anzeiger für die Altertumswissenschaft*, 7 (Vienna, 1954), pp. 65-90.

——, "Heraklits Tod," *op.cit.*, 7 (1954), pp. 250-253.

Nestle, W., "Heraklit und die Orphiker," *Philologus*, 64 (1905), pp. 367-384.

——, "War Heraklit Empiriker?" *Archiv zur Geschichte der Philosophie*, 25 (1912), pp. 275ff.

Paci, E., "La concezione mitologico-filosofico del logos in Eraclito," *Acme*, 2 (1949), pp. 176-201.

Pfleiderer, Edmund, "Die pseudoheraklitischen Briefe und ihr Verfasser," Sonder-Abdruck aus *Rheinisches Museum für Philologie*, n.s., 42.

Power, O. S., "Heraclitus, Fr. 28 Diels; a New Interpretation," *American Philological Association, Transactions and Proceedings*, 78 (1947), pp. 432-433. These are our Frs. 87 and 71.

Rabinowitz, W. Gerson, and W. I. Matson, "Heraclitus as Cosmologist," *Review of Metaphysics*, 10 (1956), pp. 244-257.

Reinhardt, Karl, "Heraclitea," *Hermes*, 77 (1942), pp. 225-248.

——, "Heraklits Lehre vom Feuer," *Hermes*, 77 (1942), pp. 1-27.

Robertson, D. S., "On the Story of Heraclitus told by Aristotle in *De Partibus Animalium*," Cambridge (Eng.) Philological Society, 1938.

Schultz, Wolfgang, "Die Kosmologie des Rauchopfers nach Fr. 67," *Archiv zur Geschichte der Philosophie*, 22 (1909), pp. 197-229. This is our Fr. 121.

Snell, Bruno, "Die Sprache Heraklits," *Hermes*, 61 (1926), pp. 353-381.

——, "Heraklits Fragment 10," *Hermes*, 76 (1941), pp. 84-87. On Fr. 112.

Spengler, Oswald, "Heraklit," in his *Reden und Aufsätze* (Munich, 1951).

Stefanini, L., "In nascita del logos in Eraclito," *Giornale critico della filosofia italiana*, 5 (1951), pp. 1-24.

Tannery, Paul, "Héraclite et le concept de Logos," *Revue philosophique*, 16 (1883), pp. 292ff.

Vernenius, W. J., "Psychological Statement of Heraclitus," *Mnemosyne*, Series III (1943).

Vlastos, Gregory, "On Heraclitus," *American Journal of Philology*, 76 (1955), pp. 337-368.

Wolf, E., "Der Ursprung des abendländischen Rechtsgedankens bei Anaximander und Heraklit," *Symposium*, 1 (1948), pp. 35-87.

Wundt, M., "Die Philosophie des Heraklit von Ephesus im Zusammenhang mit der Kultur Ioniens," *Archiv zur Geschichte der Philosophie*, 20 (1907).

Ziller, W., "Zu einigen Fragm. der heraklitischen Physik," *Rheinisches Museum*, 62 (1907), pp. 54-60.

Zoumpos, A. N., "Die metaphysische Bedeutung des Wortes Ἀίδης bei Herakleitos," *Actes du XIème congrès international de philosophie*, 12 (1953), pp. 34-55.

5. BOOKS AND ARTICLES ON RELATED SUBJECTS

Adam, James, *The Religious Teachers of Greece* (Edinburgh, 1908).

——, *The Vitality of Platonism* (Cambridge, Eng., 1911). Chapter III: "The Doctrine of the Logos of Heraclitus."

All, Anthony, *Geschichte der Logosidee* (Leipzig, 1896).

Anrich, Gustav, *Das antike Mysterienwesen in seinen Einfluss auf das Christenbild* (Göttingen, 1894).

Baeumker, Clemens, *Das Problem der Materie in der griechischen Philosophie* (Münster, 1890).

Bapp, Karl, *Aus Goethes griechischen Gedankenwelt* (Leipzig, 1921).

Barie, G. T., *L'esigenza unitaria da Talete a Platone* (Milan, 1931).

Beare, W., *Greek Theories of Elementary Cognition* (Oxford, 1906).

Brandon, S. G. F., *Time and Mankind; an historical and philosophical study of mankind's attitude to the phenomena of change* (London, 1951).

Buber, Martin, "What Is Common to All," *Review of Metaphysics*, 11 (1958), pp. 359-379.

Burnet, John, *Early Greek Philosophy* (London, 1892; 4th edition, 1920).

Calogero, Guido, *Studi sull' eleatismo* (Rome, 1932).

Capelle, Wilhelm, *Die griechische Philosophie*, 3 vols. (Berlin, 1922-1924): Vol. 1.

———, *Die Vorsokratiker* (Leipzig, 1935).

Chauvet, Emmanuel, *La philosophie des médicins grecs* (Paris, 1886).

Cherniss, Harold, *Aristotle's Criticism of Presocratic Philosophers* (Baltimore, 1935).

———, "The Characteristics and Effects of Presocratic Philosophy," *Journal of the History of Ideas*, 12 (1951), pp. 319-345.

Cornford, Francis M., *From Religion to Philosophy* (1912).

———, *The Laws of Motion in Ancient Thought* (Cambridge, Eng., 1931).

———, "Mystery Religions and Pre-Socratic Philosophy," *The Cambridge Ancient History*, 4 (1926), pp. 522-578.

———, *The Origins of Greek Philosophical Thought* (Cambridge, Eng., 1952).

Croissant, Jeanne, "Matière et changement dans la physique ionienne," *Antiquité classique*, 13 (1944), pp. 61-94.

Deichgräber, Karl, "Hymnische Elemente in der philosophischen Prosa der Vorsokratoker," *Philologus*, 88 (1933), pp. 347-361.

Delatte, A., *Les conceptions de l'enthousiasme chez les philosophes présocratiques* (Paris, 1934).

Diès, A., *Le cycle mystique: la divinité, origine et fin des existences individuelles dans la philosophique antésocratique* (Paris, 1909).

Dodds, E. R., *The Greeks and the Irrational* (Berkeley, 1951).

Eliade, Mircea, *The Myth of the Eternal Return* (Eng. tr., New York, 1954).

Fairbanks, Arthur, *The First Philosophers of Greece* (New York, 1898).

Freeman, Kathleen, *The Pre-Socratic Philosophers* (Oxford, 1946).

Friedrich, Carl, *Hippokratische Untersuchungen* (Berlin, 1899).

Garcia Bacca, Juan David, *Los Presocráticos* (Mexico City, 1944).

Gentile, M., *La metafisica presofistica* (Padua, 1939).

Gigon, Olof, *Der Ursprung der griechischen Philosophie von Hesiod bis Parmenides* (Basel, 1945).

Gilbert, Otto, *Griechische Religions-Philosophie* (Leipzig, 1911).

Gomperz, Theodor, *Greek Thinkers* (Eng. tr., 1901), Vol. I.

Guérin, P., *L'idée de justice dans la conception de l'univers chez les premiers philosophes grecs de Thalès à Héraclite* (Paris, 1934).

Hack, Roy Kenneth, *God in Greek Philosophy to the Time of Socrates* (Princeton, 1931).

Heidegger, Martin, *Einführung in die Metaphysik* (Tübingen, 1953): esp. pp. 96-103, 127, 130, 146.

――――, "Aletheia," *Vorträge und Aufsätze* (Pfullingen, 1954), pp. 257-282. On Fr. 73.

Heidel, W. A., *Hippocratica*, 1: Harvard Studies in Classical Philology, 25 (1914).

――――, "On Certain Fragments of the Presocratics," *American Academy of Arts and Sciences, Proceedings*, 48 (1913), pp. 681-734.

――――, "On *Physis*; A Study of the Conception of Nature among the Pre-Socratics," *American Academy of Arts and Sciences, Proceedings*, 45 (1910), pp. 79-133.

――――, "Qualitative Change in Pre-Socratic Philosophy," *Archiv zur Geschichte der Philosophie*, 19 (1906), pp. 333-379.

Heinze, Max, *Die Lehre vom Logos in der griechischen Philosophie* (Oldenburg, 1872).

Hirzel, R., *Themis, Dike und Verwandtes* (Leipzig, 1907).

Huit, Charles, *La philosophie de la nature chez les ancients* (Paris, 1901).

Inge, William, "Logos," *Hastings' Encyclopaedia of Religion and Ethics.*

Jaeger, Werner, *Paideia* (Eng. tr., New York, 1943), Vol. I.

――――, *Theology in the Early Greek Philosophers* (Eng. tr., Cambridge, Mass., 1947).

Joel, Karl, *Geschichte der antiken Philosophie* (Tübingen, 1921), Vol. I.

――――, *Der Ursprung der Naturphilosophie aus dem Geiste der Mystik* (Jena, 1906).

Kafka, G., *Die Vorsokratiker* (Basel, 1948).

Kirk, Geoffrey S., "The Problem of Cratylus," *American Journal of Philology*, 72 (1951), pp. 225-252.

――――, and J. E. Raven, *The Presocratic Philosophers* (Cambridge, Eng., 1957).

Kranz, Walther, *Kosmos und Mensch in der Vorstellung des frühen Griechentums* (Göttingen, 1938).

Maddalena, Antonio, *Sulla cosmologia ionica da Talete ad Eraclito* (Padua, 1941).

McClure, Matthew T.: see Lattimore in Section 2 of Bibliography.

Mondolfo, Rodolfo, *L'infinito nel pensiero dei greci* (Florence, 1934).

Mugler, Ch., *Deux thèmes de la cosmologie grecque; devenir cyclique et pluralité des mondes* (Paris, 1953).

Navarro Monzó, Julio, *La Búsqueda Presocrática* (Montevideo, 1926).

Nestle, Wilhelm, *Vom Mythos zum Logos* (Stuttgart, 1940).

Nietzsche, Friedrich, "Die Philosophie im tragischen Zeitalter der Griechen," *Werke* (1896), Vol. 10.

Oehler, Richard, *Nietzsches Verhältnis zur vorsokratischen Philosophie* (Halle, 1903).

Onians, R. B., *The Origins of European Thought about the Body, the Mind, the Soul, the World, Time and Fate* (Cambridge, Eng., 1951).

Palme, Adolf, *Studien zur hippokratischen Schrift, περὶ διαίτης* (Tübingen, 1933).

Patin, Alois, "Parmenides im Kampfe gegen Heraklit," *Jahrbuch für die klassische Philosophie*, 25 (1899), pp. 491-660.

Reinhardt, Karl, *Parmenides und die Geschichte der griechischen Philosophie* (Bonn, 1916).

Rey, Abel, *La science dans l'antiquité* (Paris, 1930-1948), Vol. 11.

Rivaud, Albert, *La principe du devenir et la notion de la matière dans la philosophie grecque depuis les origines jusqu'à Theophraste* (Paris, 1906).

Rohde, Erwin, *Psyche; the Cult of Souls and Belief in Immortality among the Greeks* (Eng. tr., 1925).

Rosenstock-Huessy, Eugen, *Soziologie*, Vol. 11, "Die Vollzahl der Zeiten" (Stuttgart, 1958).

———, *Zurück in das Wagnis der Sprache* (Berlin, 1957).

Rousseaux, A., *Le monde classique* (Paris, 1951). Contains a study of Heraclitus.

Schmidt, P., "Geist und Lehre," *Eranos-Jahrbuch*, 13 (1945), pp. 133-185.

Sciacca, M. F., *Studi sulla filosofia antica* (Naples, 1935).

Scoon, Robert, *Greek Philosophy before Plato* (Princeton, 1928).

Snell, Bruno, "Die Ausdrücke für den Begriff des Wissens in der vorplatonischen Philosophie," *Philosophische Untersuchungen,* Heft 29 (Berlin, 1924).

———, *The Discovery of Mind; the Greek Origins of European Thought* (Cambridge, Mass., 1953).

Stefanini, L., *Il preimaginismo dei greci: Pitagora, Eraclito, Parmenide, Gorgia* (Padua, 1953).

Szabo, A., "Zum Verständnis der Eleaten," *Acta Antiqua Academiae Scientiarum Hungaricae,* 2 (Budapest, 1953-1954), pp. 243-289. Argues that Parmenides' philosophy arose by way of reaction to that of Heraclitus.

Tannery, Paul, *Pour l'histoire de la science hellène* (Paris, 1887).

Teichmüller, Gustav, *Neue Studien zur Geschichte der Begriffe* (Gotha, 1876-1879).

Vasconcelos, José, *Pitágoras: una Teoría del Ritmo* (Mexico City, 1921).

Vlastos, Gregory, "Equality and Justice in Early Cosmologies," *Classical Philology,* 42 (1947), pp. 156-178.

von Fritz, Kurt, "νοῦς, νοεῖν, and their Derivatives in Pre-Socratic Philosophy, 1: From the Beginning to Parmenides," *Classical Philology,* 40 (1945), pp. 223-242.

Weerts, Emil, *Plato und der Heraklitismus* (Leipzig, 1931).

Wilamowitz-Moellendorf, U. V., "Lesefrüchte," *Hermes,* 62 (1927), pp. 276-298.

Wolf, Erik, "Der Ursprung des abendländischen Rechtsgedankens bei Anaximander und Heraklit," *Symposion,* 1 (1948), pp. 35-87.

Zeller, Edouard, *A History of Greek Philosophy from the Earliest Period to the Time of Socrates* (Eng. tr., London, 1881). Vol. II, pp. 1-116 of the English edition is devoted to Heraclitus.

GENERAL INDEX

abstraction, 13f, 20, 32-34, 42
activity, *see* process
Aeneid, 88
Aenesidemus, 48, 123
Aëtius, 43, 45, 123, 125, 143
afterlife, *see* survival
air, 6, 40, 47-49, 123
Alcmaeon, 101, 119, 128
Alexander (the Aristotelian), 40, 121
anachronism, 113
Anaxagoras, 102
Anaximander, 4-6, 40, 92f, 113
Anaximenes, 4, 6, 32, 39f, 46, 113, 121, 123
anthropomorphism, 7, 72f, 96f
appearance, 4-6, 26, 30f, 40
Aristarchus, 148
aristocratism, 11f, 22, 85f
Aristophanes, 150
Aristotle, 16, 20, 33-35, 40-42, 54f, 59, 62f, 74, 86, 108, 113f, 116, 118, 120-122, 124f, 127, 129, 134, 138f, 142-145, 147, 150, 156
Arius Didymus, 63, 126, 144
Asclepius, 91, 121, 128
athleticism (intellectual), 27
authenticity, 17, 130-134
authority, 21, 51-54
Aztecs, 50

Bacon, Francis, 7, 20, 116f
Bailey, Cyril, 43, 122f
balance, 3, 51, 107. *See also* harmony
banishment, 11, 84
barbarism, spiritual, 26, 119
barley drink, 58, 64f
battle, death in, 86, 127
beginning, *see* generation
Bergson, Henri, 49
Berkeley, George, 20
Bible, 132
biography, 10-12
birth, 47, 57, 84
blood, 69
boundless, cosmic, 5, 93, 113
bow, 85, 91, 100, 108
Boyle, Robert, 122
breath, 6, 63, 113f

burial, 11, 137
Burnet, John, 21f, 56, 85, 106f, 113f, 132, 154
Butcher, S. H., 127
byrsa, 88, 128
Bywater, Ingram, 35, 77, 112, 124; App. B, *passim*

Carthage, 88
cause, 4, 20, 39, 41
ceremony, religious, 10f, 69
Chaldeans, 50
chance, 35f, 75, 80, 104, 120f
change, *see* process
Cherniss, Harold, 56, 122, 124f
Chesterton, Gilbert K., 98
child, 29, 31, 36, 66, 104f, 133
China, 3, 16
Christ, 95, 98
Christianity, 71, 75, 98, 132f
chronology, 3-6
circle, 90, 99-101
city, 83, 88f, 128
Clement of Alexandria, 23, 45, 75, 80, 131f, 134-139, 141f, 145-150, 154, 156
clothes, 126f
coalescence, 11-16, 26-28, 74, 113, 118, 144f. *See also* participation
Coleridge, Samuel T., 118
coming-to-be, 30, 47, 120. *See also* generation
common awareness, 19f, 24f, 83, 89, 100
community, 9f, 83-89
concretion, 9f, 31, 40, 42. *See also* quality
condensation, 6, 45
conflagration, cosmic, 48, 50-56, 81f, 124, 139
cosmology, 3, 6, 34-36, 41-43, 47, 61, 65, 104, 107-110, 119, 124
Crotona, 8
cycles, cosmic, 50-56, 101, 124f, 139, 141

death, 11, 20, 47, 74-80, 89, 108, 137, 144f
dedication, of scrolls, 12, 115f

Delphi, 20, 115f
delusion, 27, 65, 83, 103, 117
Democritus, 42, 93, 102
depth, semantic, 94
Descartes, René, 20
destiny, 35f, 81, 89, 120
dharma, 118
dialectic, 15, 20
Dido, 88
Diels, Hermann (including Diels-Kranz), 17, 35, 103f, 112-115, 124, 134, 156; App. B, *passim*
Diogenes Laertius, 10f, 113f, 135f, 143, 145, 148f, 155f
Dionysus, 69, 88
distance, spiritual, 8, 11, 85, 115
downward way, 46, 49, 53, 66, 81, 86, 125
doxography, 17, 63, 130-134, 138
dream, 20, 27, 78, 137
dryness, 26, 32, 62, 65, 79, 109, 126, 144. *See also* fire
dualism, 15, 37, 103-105

earth, 6, 37, 125
efflux, 46, 123
Eleaticism, 8-10
elements, natural, 37, 39, 47f
Eliade, Mircea, 123
Empedocles, 52f, 104, 120, 124
Empson, William, 127
Ephesus, 10, 84
Epicharmus, 23f, 119f
Epicurus, 43, 122f
epistemology, 13, 15, 31-34, 41, 117f, 119
Erinyes, 102
eschatology, 61, 66f, 74-81, 126f, 146
eternity, 30, 35, 54, 75f, 101, 139, 141
etymology, treatise on, 153
Eudoxus, 116
Euripides, 69, 126
Eustathius, 115
evaporation, 45-47, 62, 125, 143f
evidence, 19f, 51-54, 130-134

Fairbanks, Arthur, 61, 76, 85, 107, 132
fire, 9, 25, 27, 30, 37-57, 62, 64, 78f,

81f, 93, 106, 121f, 124f, 126, 140f, 144
first principle, 4-8, 14, 30, 33f, 39-42, 55, 64, 69-71, 84, 87, 92, 96f, 104, 110, 124
fools, 58, 83, 85. *See also* downward way
four elements, 33, 37, 39, 47-49
Fränkel, Hermann, 56, 106, 128, 155
Freeman, Kathleen, 61, 107, 113, 132
Freud, Sigmund, 89, 95, 98

Galenus, 47, 123, 142f, 149
Galileo, 41
generation, cosmic, 41, 54, 57
Gigon, Olof, 56, 87, 127
gnomic writings, 7
God, 3, 7f, 57, 69, 71-73, 90, 96, 110, 125
gods, 7, 34, 73-76
Goethe, J. W. von, 14, 44, 118
gold, 19, 37, 90, 122
Gomperz, Theodor, 56, 131
grammar, 13f, 104, 132
Great Year, 50f. *See also* cycles
Greece, 3f, 12
Greek language, 13f, 43f, 141, 143
Greek thought, 4, 17, 41f
gymnastic style, 91

Hades, 59, 66, 69, 126
harmony, 25, 27, 36, 102, 107-110, 129, 140
Hastings' Encyclopaedia, 103
Heidel, W. A., 122
Helicon, Mount, 115f
Heraclitus the grammarian, 152
Hermadorus, 11, 84
Hesiod, 3, 46, 84, 91
Hicks, R. D., 114
Hippasus, 9, 56, 114
Hippolytus, 25f, 41, 75, 80, 122, 128, 134, 136, 139-142, 147, 149-156
Homer, 29, 46, 52, 83, 124, 129, 140
Homeric hymns, 3
horse, wooden, 128
hybris, 5, 85f

Iamblichus, 9, 137
identity, 26, 35, 101, 110, 120

idols (Baconian), 7, 9, 13, 116f
igneus turbo, 43
illness, 11
illusion, *see* delusion, perception
image-idea, 14
immortality, 75f, 126f. *See also* survival
impulse, 49f, 57f, 65
India, 3, 16, 50
influence, 8-10, 46, 75, 114
innuendo, 18, 27, 137
intelligence, 15, 25, 41, 68, 71, 102, 104, 107. *See also* mind
interpretation, 12f, 17f, 21-24, 80, 116f, 130-134, 136, 139, 141
intoxication, 58, 84
Ionia, 4-8, 121
Iran, 3, 16, 50
irresponsibility, cosmic, 35, 66, 73, 139
Isaiah, 3
Israel, 3
Italy, 8

justice, 5, 13, 29, 68, 110, 113, 127

Kant, Immanuel, 20
Keats, John, 118. *See also* negative capability
Kirk, Geoffrey S., 24, 44, 51-53, 56, 79f, 87, 107, 120, 122f, 127, 135, 153f
knowledge, 19-26, 104f. *See also* perception; truth

language, 13f, 22-24, 26, 33f, 59-61, 63, 74-77, 105
Lao-tze, 3
Lattimore, Richmond, 61, 107
law, physical, 49; political, 83, 87f, 127f
Leucippus, 42, 93, 102
Liddell and Scott, 87, 138
life-cycle, 5, 47, 91
light, 25, 38, 68, 77-81, 144, 146
lightning-flash, 37, 43f, 123
Locke, John, 20
locomotion, 41, 43, 122
logic, 15, 20, 24, 27, 33f, 41, 63, 105, 117

Logos, 19-25, 51, 57, 68, 71, 87, 102, 107, 117, 119f, 126, 135, 154
love, 97, 124
Lucian, 139
Lucretius, 43f, 123
lyre, 85, 102, 108, 117, 129

manifold, 4, 8, 26, 30-35, 41, 45, 51, 113, 124f
Marcus Aurelius, 109, 129, 137, 146, 156
Martin, Everett D., 117
mathematics, 9
matter, 4, 39f, 63, 114, 126. *See also* elements; four elements
Maximus of Tyre, 142, 156
Mayas, 50
Mayer, Gottfried, 115
measure, 42
mechanical principle, 122
memory, 70
metaphor, 25, 71-73, 78, 81, 94-99
metaphysics, 5, 8, 23, 33f, 69-73, 93, 103-110, 120, 122, 124, 129
method, 12, 17, 19-28, 116f
Miletus, school of, 4, 6, 8, 39, 45f
mind, 7, 69, 135; cosmic, 41, 44, 49, 69-71, 73, 102-110
misanthropy, 11, 84
moisture, 32, 45, 61-64, 109
Mondolfo, Rudolfo, 56
motion, 6, 65, 128. *See also* locomotion; process
music, 108f
mysticism, 124-127
mythology, 4, 7, 40, 171f

Nahm, Milton C., 132
nature, 4-6, 37-57, 93, 116, 120
Navarro Monzo, Julio, 21
necessity, 35f, 121
negative capability, 16, 39, 118
Nietzsche, Friedrich, 115. *See also* distance
Noëtus, 133
Numenius, 144

objectivism, 12, 15, 21, 23, 30, 73, 119
obscurity, 12, 16, 93, 116, 133
Oedipus, 127

ontology, 4-6, 13, 16, 31, 39, 44, 122
opposites, 5f, 26, 33, 120, 140. *See also* paradox; tension
Origen, 140, 146, 148, 151, 156
Orphic sayings, 3f, 113

paradox, 10, 12-16, 26, 33, 66, 78, 94-98, 100, 108f, 147
Parmenides, 9f, 15, 103f, 115
participation, 21, 24f, 71, 119. *See also* coalescence
particulars, 21. *See also* manifold
Patrick, G. T. W., 151
Paul, St., 114
Pausanias, 116
perception, 6, 26, 31, 59, 63, 65-67, 118, 138. *See also* epistemology
periodicity, *see* cycles
perspective, 5, 27, 46, 62, 82, 86, 121, 151
pessimism, 11f, 115
Pfleiderer, Edmund, 108
Phaedo, 76, 126f, 128f
Philo, 137
philosophy, idea of, 23f, 32. *See also* truth; wisdom
physics, 6, 37-57, 120, 122, 124
Plato, 3, 9, 16, 20, 27, 52-54, 76, 93, 123, 127, 137f, 150, 155f
Plotinus, 139, 149, 156
plurisignation, 78, 127
Plutarch, 45, 47, 56, 120, 123f, 137, 140, 142f, 145f, 148f, 152f, 155f
pneuma, 118
Poetics (Aristotle), 127-129
Polybius, 136, 156
polytheism, 7, 74f
Porphyrius, 144, 151f, 156
potentiality, 5, 113, 126
prayer, 69f
process, 3-6, 13-15, 27, 29-36, 63, 75, 93, 105, 120, 125, 138f, 142; *et passim*
Proclus, 137, 156
prophetic role, 22, 69
Pseudo-Aristotle, 41, 112, 116, 125
pun, 27, 77, 127, 147
purity, 122, 155
pyramids, 42, 122
Pythagoras, school of, 8f, 27, 84, 93, 107-109, 114f, 119

qualities, 5f, 13-15, 31-34, 42, 65, 129
quantity, 6, 122, 141

rarefaction, 6. *See also* upward way
Raven, J. E., 24, 120
reason, *see* Logos; mind; intelligence
religion, 10, 16, 68-82
river, 29f, 37, 90, 142, 152
Rodin, Auguste, 39
Rouse, W. H. D., 116

Schleiermacher, Friedrich, 14, 17, 135, 160
Schopenhauer, Arthur, 11, 19, 115
science, 4-6, 32, 37-56, 119
sculpture, 39
self, *see* soul
self-assertion, *see* hybris
self-examination, 19, 27
semantics, 13-17, 31-34, 77f, 122, 127. *See also* paradox
Seneca, 43, 149, 152
Sextus Empiricus, 134f, 136f, 146, 156
Shakespeare, William, 118
Sibyl, 69
Simplicius, 40, 42, 56, 74, 140
sleep, 27, 69f, 78f, 129, 137
smell, 59, 66, 126, 145f
Smith, J. A., 126
smoke, 59, 66
Sophocles, 15
soul, 6, 59-69, 70f, 75-77, 79f, 109, 119, 126, 129
Spengler, Oswald, 37f, 121
Spinoza, Baruch, 20
Stobaeus, 119, 124, 135f, 144f, 147f, 150, 156
Stocks, J. L., 56, 124
Stoicism, 50, 54, 109, 123
Strabo, 113, 143, 146, 150, 156
strife, 35, 53, 120, 133
subject-object, *see* epistemology
Suidas, 114
survival, 74-80, 118, 126, 146f
symbol, 14, 30, 38f, 66, 122
Symmachus, 149
synecdoche, 44

tao, 110, 118
Tao Teh Ching, 16, 110
Teichmüller, Gustav, 39
tension, 10, 27, 85, 104, 108, 140
Tertullian, 116, 143, 151
Thales, 4, 39f, 45, 74, 92f, 126
Theaetetus, 21f
theater, idols of, 13, 116f, 122
Themistius, 137
theology, 69-74
Theophrastus, 39, 65, 126, 143, 145, 156
time, 5f, 30, 36, 50f, 139
tragedy, 86, 127, 129
transcendence, 7, 23f, 73, 102-110, 119, 129
triadicity, 33f, 120
Trinity, doctrine of, 133
Troy, 88, 128
truth, 21, 23-25, 93, 110, 154
Tzetzes, 139, 150

unguents, 106, 155
universal, 20, 22, 93
Upanishads, 3, 16
upward way, 6, 12, 49, 53, 81, 86, 102, 109, 125, 128
usurpation, 127

vanishing, 29f, 120, 142
Vergil, 88, 127f
Vita Homeri, 149
von Hartmann, Eduard, 49

wall, city, 88, 128
Walzer, Richard, 132, 134; App. B, *passim*
war, *see* strife
way up and down, 6, 45, 80, 108, 139. *See also* downward way; upward way
wisdom, 3, 11, 15, 20, 23f, 38, 70f, 89
Word, *see* Logos
word-magic, 24
world cycles, *see* cycles

Xenocrates, 116
Xenophanes, 7f, 41, 72, 114, 126

Zarathustra, 3
Zeller, Edouard, 10, 56, 125
Zend-Avesta, 116
Zeus, 69, 102, 105f, 110, 120
Zoroaster, *see* Zarathustra

INDEX OF PRINCIPAL GREEK WORDS

Page numbers are indicated by roman type and Fragment numbers by italic.

ἄγαλμα, 75
ἀγαθός, 91, 99, 106
ἀγών, 93
ἄδικος, 106
ἀεί, 138; 29, 43
ἀήρ, 123; 34
ἀθάνατος, 66
Ἄιδης, Ἄιδης, 59, 77
αἷμα, 78
αἰνικτής, 116
αἰσθητός, 138
αἴτιον, 121, 122, 141; 30
αἰών, 139; 24
ἀκοή, 11
ἀλήθεια, 128
ἀληθής, 10
ἀμαθίη, 53
ἀμαρτάνω, 129
ἁμάρτημα, 127
ἀμαρτία, 86, 108, 127, 129
ἀμοιβή, 141
ἀνάγκη, 36, 120
ἀναθυμίασις, 45, 62, 143-144; 43
ἀναθυμιάω, 44
ἀναπαύομαι, 23, 97
ἀνάπαυσις, 99
ἄναξ, 18
ἀνέλπιστος, 131, 137, 138; 19
ἄνεμμα, 142
ἀνήρ, 3, 48, 95, 105
ἀνθρώπειος, 61, 81
ἄνθρωπος, 25, 29, 62, 65, 67, 69, 86, 101, 104, 106
ἀνταμοιβή, 141; 28
ἀντίξουν, 98
ἄνω, 128; 108
ἀξύνετος, 55
ἀοιδός, 91
ἄπαντα, 125; 28, 29, 85, 94
ἄπειρον, τό, 113
ἀπιστίη, 63
ἅπτω, 68, 78; 65
ἀρετή, 10
ἄριστος, 86; 46, 84, 85
ἄρκτος, 39

ἁρμονία, 107, 129; 98, 116, 117
ἁρμόζω, 153
ἀρχή, 40, 101, 113, 121; 109
Ἀρχίλοχος, 93
ἀσωματώτατος, 43
ἀτύχημα, 127
αὐγή, 144
αὐός, 46
ἀφανής, 116

βάκχος, 76
βάρβαρος, 13
βασιλεύς, 25
βασιληίη, 24
βίος, 100, 153; 66, 115
βιός, 100, 153
βλάξ, 54
βουλή, 83

γένεσις, 120
γῆ, 32, 33, 34, 49
γίγνομαι, 124, 125; 1, 26, 49, 52, 98, 124
γνάφειος, 111
γνώμη, 61, 120

δαίμων, 69, 105
Δελφοί, 18
δῆμος, 82, 91
διαφέρω, 129
δίκαιος, 106
δίκη, 113; 26, 71, 100, 122
διοίκησις, 122
Διόνυσος, 77
δοκέω, 57, 67, 87
δόκιμος, 87
δόξα, 128
δοῦλος, 25
δῦνον, 73

ἐγείρω, 16
ἐγρηγορέω, 15, 65
εἰκῆ, 5
εἱμαρμένη, 120

εἶναι (used existentially), 115, 124;
  1, 2, 29
εἰρήνη, 121
ἔκποια, 123
ἔκπύρωσις, 50, 52, 53, 54, 124
ἐκπυροῦμαι, 124
ἔλπομαι, 67
ἔλπητος, 131
ἐλπίζω, 132, 137, 138; 19
ἔμφρων, 126
ἕν, 128; 83, 84, 112, 114
ἐναντίος, 140
ἕνεκα, 143
ἔνυλος, 126
ἔξαψις, 143
ἐξευρίσκω, 138; 19, 122
ἐπίνοια, 122
Ἐρινύες, 122
ἔρις, 140; 26, 98
Ἑρμόδορος, 95
εὕδω, 16, 65
εὐθύς (adj.), 111
εὔχομαι, 75
Ἐφέσιος, 95, 96

Ζεύς, 120; 39, 119

ἡδονή, 121
ἦθος, 61, 69
ἥλιος, 36, 37, 38, 122
ἡμέρα, 36, 94, 121
ἥρως, 75
Ἡσίοδος, 94

θάλασσα, 32, 33, 101
θάνατος, 16, 34, 47, 49, 66, 118. See
  also 67
θεῖος, 128; 61, 63, 81
θεός, 25, 29, 126; 74, 75, 79, 86, 104,
  106, 121
θνητός, 66
θυμός, 51
θύωμα, 155; 121

ἰατρός, 107
ἴδιος, 15
ἱερός, 56
ἰχθύς, 101

καθαίρω, 78
καθεύδω, 14; 124

κάματος, 89, 99
καπνός, 58
καρφαλέος, 22
καταλαμβάνω, 71, 72
κάτω, 108
κεραυνός, 123; 35
κινέομαι, 43, 50
κίνησις, 122, 126
κλέος, 85
κοινός, 135; 2, 15
κόπρος, 60
κόρος, 30, 99, 121
κόσμος, 122, 124, 141; 15, 29, 40, 124
κρίνω, 72
κρύπτω, 17
κυβερνάω, 120
κυκεών, 50
κύκλος, 128; 109
κύων, 90

λέγω, 21, 119, 120, 138; 18
λιμός, 99, 121
λογικός, 62
λογισμός, 120√   √
λόγος, 21, 22, 23, 63, 92, 118, 119,
  120, 126; 1, 2, 7, 33, 42, 45, 54,
  64, 118
λύρα(-η), 117

μάγος, 76
μάθησις, 11
μαίνομαι, 78, 79
μαντεῖον, 18
μάρτυρ, 12, 13
μέσα, 113
μεταβάλλω, 23
μέτρον, 141; 29, 122
μισθός, 107
μοῖρα, 70
μόρος, 70, 97
μυέω, 76
μυστήριον, 76

νεκρός, 68
νέκυς, 60
νήπιος, 105
νοετός, 126
νόμος, 87; 81, 82, 83
νόος, 120; 6, 81, 91
νόσος, 56
νοῦσος, 99

ξὺν νῷ, 120; *81*
ξυνός, 100, 120, 134, 144; *2, 26, 80,*
81

ὁδός, *108, III*
οἴησις, *56*
οἰκίζω, *35*
οἶνος, *53*
οἷς, ὦτα, *12, 13*
ὅλος, 122
Ὅμηρος, *92, 93*
ὁμολογέω, 154; *118*
ὄν, 48, 123. See also εἶναι
ὄνομα, 100, 115, 119
ὄνος, *102*
οὐσία, 121
ὀφθαλμός, *12, 13*
ὄψις, *11, 65*

πάθος, 126
παῖς, *24, 48, 97, 105*
πάλιν, 124, 126; *31*
παλίντονος, 154
παλίντροπος, 115, 153; *117*
πᾶν, πάντα, 113, 124, 125; *1, 7, 20,*
25, 26, 28, 35, 41, 58, 72, 98, 112,
118, 120, 123. See also ἅπαντα
πάντα διὰ πάντα 104; *120*
πάντες, *80, 81*
πέλω, 115
πέρας, 101; *109*
περιέχω, 118, 128; *62*
περιφέρεια, *109*
πίθηκος, *104*
πιστεύω, 132
πληγή, *41*
πλοῦτος, *96*
πνεῦμα, 114
πόλεμος, 120, 140; *26*
πόλις, *81*
πολλά, τά, *63*
πολλοί, οἱ, *2, 57, 85, 91*
πολυμαθίη, *6*
πομπή, *77*
πονηρεύομαι, *96*
ποταμός, *21, 110, 121*
προειρημένον, 118
πῦρ, 122, 124, 125, 141; *28, 29, 32,*
34, 72

ῥέω, 138; *20, 43*
ῥῖνες, *58*

σάρμα, *40*
σβέννυμι, 88
σβέσις, 143
σῆμα, 137
σημαίνω, 137; *18*
Σίβυλλα, *79*
σκολιός, 99; *III*
σκοτεινός, 116
σοφία, *104*
σοφός, 23; *7, 46, 118, 119, 120*
στοιχεῖον, 113
συμμένω, 126
συμφέρω, *112*
συνᾷδον, *112*
συνάψιες, *112*
συνεργός, *124*
συνίστημι, 124
σύρμα, *102*
σώζω, 126
σῶμα, 122, 124
σωματικός, 121
σωφρονέω, 136; *9, 10*

τεῖχος, *82*
τελευτή, 113
τέλος, 101
τίσις, 113
τόξον, 115, *117*
τύραννος, 127

ὕβρις, 88. See also hybris in General
Index
ὑγιείη, 99
ὑγρός, *22, 44, 47, 48*
ὕδωρ, *34, 49, 101*
ὑλικός, 121
ὕμνος, *77*
ὕπνος, *16*

φάος, *65*
φθείρ, *92*
φθορά, 120
φιλόσοφος, 23, 135; *3*
φρενήρης, *62*
φρονέω, 136; *80*
φρόνησις, 135; *2*
φρόνιμος, 122
φρήν, *91*
φύλαξ, *68*
φυσιολογία, 113
φύσις, 113, 134; *1, 10, 17*
φύω, 113

CPSIA information can be obtained
at www.ICGtesting.com
Printed in the USA
BVHW061022101118
532635BV00002B/211/P

9 780282 524210